THREE IN THIRTEEN

The Story of a Mosquito Night Fighter Ace

Roger Dunsford
with
Geoff Coughlin

☽ CASEMATE
Oxford & Philadelphia

Published in Great Britain and
the United States of America in 2017 by
CASEMATE PUBLISHERS
The Old Music Hall, 106–108 Cowley Road, Oxford OX4 1JE, UK
and
1950 Lawrence Road, Havertown, PA 19083, USA

© Roger Dunsford and Geoff Coughlin 2017

Hardcover Edition: ISBN 978-1-61200-440-2
Digital Edition: ISBN 978-1-61200-441-9

A CIP record for this book is available from the British Library

Printed in the United Kingdom by TJ International

For a complete list of Casemate titles, please contact:

CASEMATE PUBLISHERS (UK)
Telephone (01865) 241249
Fax (01865) 794449
Email: casemate-uk@casematepublishers.co.uk
www.casematepublishers.co.uk

CASEMATE PUBLISHERS (US)
Telephone (610) 853-9131
Fax (610) 853-9146
Email: casemate@casematepublishing.com
www.casematepublishing.com

Contents

Author's Note:
Roger Dunsford

I met Joe Singleton, briefly, in the early nineties when I went with his son, Pete, and our wives to Joe and Theresa's home in Weston Turville on the edge of the Chilterns. My memory is of a charming, quietly spoken gentleman in the truest sense of that word. Our conversation centred on his genuine curiosity about my experiences as a pilot in the (then) present day air force. I was vaguely aware, from previous conversations with Pete, that he had been a Mosquito pilot and had a pretty distinguished war record, but that was about all and, somehow, we never got around to talking about that very much. The Singletons were and are a pretty self-effacing lot. Joe died in December 1996 and I now very much regret my lack of curiosity at our only meeting – oh, how I now wish I had talked to Joe about his experiences.

I first met Pete Singleton in the late seventies when we were both Flight Lieutenants posted as Flight Commanders on the staff of Initial Officer Training Wing of the Royal Air Force College at Cranwell. I had arrived there after completing a Vulcan captain's tour on 44 (Rhodesia) Squadron at RAF Waddington and Pete was at a similar stage of his career as a Fighter Controller. So, he had come from the defensive and I from the offensive side of the RAF's role in the Cold War, which was then at its height. The chances of the career path of a bomber pilot crossing that of a Fighter Controller were small enough. That it should instantly lead to a friendship, still going strong after 36 years, is rare indeed. Another curiosity is that one of Pete's students back then was a certain callow youth called Chris Goss. He is now a leading expert and writer of great scholarship on WWII aviation, particularly from a Luftwaffe perspective. He has been a great help in correlating Joe's encounters with, literally, the other side of the story; thank you, Chris. Such serendipity is a persistent thread running through this book.

Pete and I both regard that tour – teaching the future leaders of the RAF about, well, leadership – as a privilege and quite possibly the most enjoyable of all tours. To this day we reminisce with much affection and belly laughs at the escapades of both staff and students during our time at Cranwell. Our respective careers diverged permanently after that, but we kept in regular touch, visited and holidayed together; our respective wives – Prue and Sandi – also became firm friends. After Pete and Sandi both retired as Wing Commanders, they eventually fulfilled a long held dream to buy land and build themselves a home in Cyprus. Needless to say, Prue and I were eager to be on the waiting list to visit them as soon as (actually before) their beautiful spread in foothills of the Troodos Mountains was finished. It was only when, during those first few visits to Cyprus and I saw Joe's boxed medals (DSO, DFC, AFC, plus campaign medals) proudly displayed on their wall alongside Chris Stothard's 'Two Down, One to Go' picture, that I realized Joe's was no ordinary war record. Gradually, after many sultry evenings and brandy sours, I prised out of Pete what he knew of Joe's wartime exploits. When Pete's memory needed refreshing on some parts of his Dad's story, he would disappear into the garage and delve into one of several large boxes of Joe's own collection of memorabilia, which Pete had had shipped out along with his medals. One day, I suggested to Pete that a significant story was hidden in these boxes and should be preserved for posterity. I cajoled him to go through the contents, which included his logbooks, combat reports, photographs, newspaper cuttings, correspondence etc. and piece together his wartime journey. I found it astonishing that, aside from the occasional mention in magazines and always just the 'Three in Thirteen Minutes' headline, the bulk of his story was largely unknown and untold. Pete wholeheartedly agreed, said he had been meaning to do it for some time and promised to get it sorted for our next visit. Several more visits came and went and still the unopened boxes lay accusingly in the corner of his garage; still Pete promised and prevaricated.

Eventually, I made a tentative enquiry as to whether he would like me to sort through the boxes on his behalf. To my surprise and delight, Pete was only too willing to accept my offer. So it was that, a month or so later, two large and heavy boxes, with contents barely touched for at least six years, arrived at the door of our home in Lincolnshire.

As will become evident, the approach I took to unravelling the plethora of jumbled information in this treasure trove was to stay on familiar ground for me – his logbooks. They provide his Service Record from the start and charted, in detail, his progress from his very first flight to the night of the 19th March 1944 and beyond (another unwritten story). It also, through often cryptic and subtle annotations made by Joe, provides insight into his private thoughts. Having specialized in night flying, wrestling with a rudimentary Terrain Following Radar, (for participation in the one and only Vulcan Night Red Flag Exercise in 1979), I had a particular interest in, and empathy with, Joe's struggles with the very earliest Air Interception Radars, when fighting in the dark.

The more I uncovered and researched Joe's journey from junior manager at Leyland Paints and Varnishes to his three kills in thirteen minutes, the more I came to appreciate that every feat of arms, such as Joe's, is the unique product of an intricate web of chance. The valour is self-evident and that is what creates the headlines. The training, skill, teamwork and technology required for success are also relatively straightforward to grasp. But the interactions of coincidences, providence, destiny, fate, fortuity – whatever you want to call it – which culminate in a man like Joe Singleton being there that night and capable of facing and achieving what he did, are barely fathomable and certainly bewitching. There are countless tales of derring-do such as Joe's already told; there are countless others either waiting to be unravelled, or hidden forever because the participants didn't make it back, physically or mentally. My sincere wish is that I have done justice to Joe Singleton's remarkable story.

It is an enormous privilege and pleasure to have been given complete and ready access to Joe's life, both written and verbal and for that I am utterly indebted to my old mate Pete Singleton. Without the encouragement, knowledge and enthusiasm of my outstanding neighbour, Geoff Coughlin, this book would never have made it to print. The skill of our graphics designer, Francis Porter, is evident in what follows; his patience with my inexpert fumblings in his world is not – thank you Francis. At an early stage of the book's development, I was exceedingly grateful to be able to discuss the trials and tribulations that lay ahead with one of my former flying instructors, Paul McDonald, whose recent excellent book – *Winged Warriors – The Cold War from the Cockpit* – has been an inspiration and proof that some old pilots, when minded to, can even write a bit.

I would also like to thank Andrea Sevier, Tim Pierce and Yvonne Potter of College Hall Library at RAF Cranwell – what a precious treasure house of Military History that is – for their invaluable assistance in researching a night fighters' world. Seb Cox is head of the Air Historical Branch at RAF Northolt and former colleague; he and his staff very kindly provided many useful links as the story unfolded. Similarly, Chris Ransted of the National Archives filled in many of the holes in the story of Joe's brush with the laws of low flying. Ewan Burnet of the RAF Museum was instrumental in preserving the delicate celluloid and tracking down the technology that enabled Joe's gun camera film, from his Bay of Biscay encounter – several stills appear in this book – to be preserved for posterity in digital form, by Martin Rogers at Prime Focus Technologies. As and when this book appears in digital format, that dramatic clip will be linked to it. Tim Allsop of DIPR in the Ministry of Defence provided confirmation that the copyrights of the Combat Reports appearing in the Appendix have expired. Finally, Steve Hinch of the Little Card Company was instrumental in my tracking down the elusive Christopher J. Stothard (Associate GAvA). Chris very generously gave his permission to use his superb painting 'Two Down One to Go' as artwork on the cover and as reproduced inside the book. Thank you Chris and thank you all.

Red Ink Logbook Entries

Joe's logbook reflects the convention at the time (and ever since) of denoting operational sorties i.e. those conducted with armed weapons or bombs in a war zone, by entering the detail in red ink. In addition, night flying sorties, which carried much greater differential from day sorties in terms of risk than today, were entered either by underlining in red ink or using red ink, in the same way as operational sorties. Today no such distinction between day and night sorties is made. In order to signify Joe's operational red ink sorties, I have adopted the convention of showing them in black, bold, italicised capitals in the text; 'normal' logbook entries are unitalicised.

Author's Note:
Geoff Coughlin

A chance meeting with Roger who showed me the great work that he had put into building and writing the wartime record of Wing Commander Joe Singleton DSO DFC AFC left me aghast! Pete Singleton, Joe's son had provided a huge amount of material from Joe's logbook to press cuttings and maps to period photographs and much more. 'This has to be published!' I told Roger, somewhat excitedly, so that people around the world can read Joe's story too and when Pete agreed, *Three in Thirteen* was born.

Most of all I am pleased for Pete, Joe's son that *Three in Thirteen* has finally been published because there is a permanent record of his father's wartime story. Like so many WWII RAF aircrew Joe's story is unique and from that first chance meeting with Roger I have always believed passionately that it should be told and it makes me very happy that this first edition is now available to all. For much the same reasons I am pleased for Roger too because of all his hard work building and writing the vast majority of the text; now it has all been brought together in one book.

Inevitably many individuals have to collaborate during any book's preparation and be willing to share their knowledge, expertise, photographs and profiles. I would like to especially thank the following for their generous support in contributing to *Three in Thirteen*:

Francis Porter (www.francisporterdesign.com) for his fantastic design capability and endless patience working with Roger and me on the design of *Three in Thirteen*;

Simon Schatz for his Junkers Ju 88 colour profile based on a line artwork by Maciej Noszczak;

Bill Dady for the remaining colour aircraft profiles you will find in *Three in Thirteen*.

Foreword

Seventy years ago today, my father, Joe Singleton, along with his navigator, Geoff Haslam, got airborne from RAF Coltishall in their Mosquito HK255. It was a very dark but starlit night and, as it turned out, a night that was to change my father's life. The confirmed destruction of three JU 188/88s within 13 minutes was an astonishing feat and one which resulted in the award of an 'immediate' DSO to my father and a DFC to Geoff. The combat, which effectively foiled a raid on Hull, was reported in the national press and Dad recorded an interview for the BBC. In his hometown of Leyland, Lancashire, he became a local hero, and I have no doubt that the people of Hull came to hear of Flight Lieutenant Joe Singleton and Flying Officer Geoff Haslam. In later years, to mark the 75th anniversary of 25 Squadron's formation, the Squadron Association commissioned a painting depicting the event as one of the proudest moments in their history. Undoubtedly, it was one of the outstanding air combats of the War.

Throughout his life, he was continually reminded of the achievement and, in later years, particularly during his retirement, he spent considerable time with historical authors and researchers. Although he was, without doubt, very proud of his war record and his DSO, he was never one to boast, and was always a bit reluctant to talk of his achievements. He did, however, always give the impression that he loved flying – especially the Mosquito – and, for him, low flying at night in enemy territory was the epitome of excitement. He and Geoff Haslam stayed firm friends throughout their lives and he also kept in touch with his earlier navigator, Brad Bradshaw. He attended 25

Squadron Association events whenever he could and was often asked to sign Mosquito prints even though the events depicted sometimes had little to do with my father's war. He was a very gentle man who was well liked and respected by those who knew him, and it is sometimes hard for me to imagine him in that cockpit.

After his death in 1996, I kept his logbooks and memorabilia and I was very happy to lend the documents to my great friend Roger Dunsford when he asked if he could have a look at them. He had met my father in the early 90s and felt that the story of 'that night' deserved a more prominent place in the public record of the history of WWII. The result is this book for which I am incredibly grateful to Roger. I commend it to you.

Wing Commander Peter M. Singleton RAF (Ret'd)
19th March 2014

Prologue:
Luxury and Luck

Many gallant actions and incredible feats of endurance are recorded, but the deeds of those who perished will never be known.[1]

Flight Lieutenant Joe Singleton could be forgiven for feeling distinctly out of his comfort zone, as he flew his Mosquito south in bright sunshine, on Saturday 5th June 1943. Since he had arrived on 25 Squadron some 18 months earlier, about half his total flying, first on Beaufighters then on Mosquitos, had been at night. More importantly, all his fighting had been in the dark including, only last month, the low-level attacks on trains in German-occupied territory. Now, at short notice, he had been given the task of leading a flight of three 25 Squadron Mosquitos, from their base at Church Fenton in Yorkshire, to support 264 Squadron, operating out of RAF Predannack in Cornwall. He had been told that their job was to support Coastal Command's anti-U-boat aircraft, by protecting them from Luftwaffe Ju 88s operating out of the Brest peninsula. There was also the chance of attacking any shipping suspected of supporting the U-boats. All of which was just fine by Joe if it had been by night, but these were to be daylight operations only. It was hard to explain to someone who had not experienced it just how different the same type of attack was, by day and by night.

At night, you relied heavily on the aircraft's radar – operated by his trusted navigator and friend Geoff Haslam, who was sitting behind him in the Mossie right now – to be your eyes and ears. Also at night, you had to concentrate on the aircraft's instruments some 18 inches from your eyes because, more often than not, that was all, or the most reliable, information you had to go on. By day, although Geoff would still be providing a great deal of support from the radar, he and Joe would have to spend most of the time with their eyes on stalks, looking out of the cockpit for a distant enemy, before the enemy spotted them. In short, night fighting was done from inside a cocoon, desperately searching for nuggets of reliable, relevant information. Day fighting was a desperate search for the same nuggets, filtered from an avalanche of information pouring into the aircraft.

Joe knew it would not take long for he and Geoff to re-acquaint themselves with daylight ops, but would they be given that luxury? The other niggle was whispered reports that the highly capable FW 190s had been spotted operating over the Bay of Biscay – a very different kettle of fish from the relatively vulnerable Ju 88s. Joe's recent elevation to Flight Commander also meant that the other two 25 Squadron crews and aircraft, were very much his responsibility. Joe may have wondered if the youth and inexperience of these four lads spared them from sharing his own misgivings – he well remembered the feelings of invincibility that prevailed, before the loss of close friends hit home.

Mid-1943 was the tipping point in the Battle of the Atlantic. New construction of merchant ships by the USA and Britain was at last approaching, by tonnage, the total losses, due primarily to German U-boats. Meanwhile, the rate at which U-boats were being sunk was beginning to outstrip Germany's ability to replace them. What Churchill described as 'the decisive phase' of the Battle was afoot.

More effective convoy techniques and defences in the north Atlantic obliged U-boat crews to take more risks, at greater range, than ever before. Whether through damage or increased sortie lengths, the U-boats had to spend an increasing proportion of their sorties on the surface for repairs, replenishment and battery charging. With five major U-boat bases in occupied France – Brest, Lorient, Saint Nazaire, La Rochelle/La Pallice and Bordeaux – the Bay of Biscay was increasingly a happy hunting ground for U-boats on or near the surface.

This played into the hands of RAF Coastal Command's 19 Group, which was markedly improving its air attack capability, with rocket and depth charge-equipped aircraft such as the Sunderland, Catalina and the American Liberator, based in the south-west of England. The Germans had converted some of their Ju 88s from light, fast bombers to maritime fighter/reconnaissance aircraft, which were taking a significant toll on the Allies' anti-submarine aircraft. To protect them, chiefly Beaufighters provided Coastal Command's air-to-air defences. As the air war over the Bay intensified, the Luftwaffe began fitting their highly effective but relatively short range FW 190s with extra fuel tanks, to take the battle out to sea, where 19 Group was causing so much damage to their U-boats. In response, Coastal Command pleaded with Bomber Harris to release some of his Mosquitos to counter the new threats. This he did with marked reluctance, after Commander-in-Chief of Coastal Command – Air Marshal John Slessor – went over Harris's head. The transit from Yorkshire to Cornwall, in the sunshine, by the three Mosquitos and crews, was one of the results.

The luxury Joe hoped for – maybe a couple of sorties to get acquainted with the area and carry out some practice daylight intercepts – was not to be. He and Geoff spent the Sunday on the ground, no doubt receiving briefings from OC 264 Squadron and picking the brains of the hard-pressed crews about Bay of Biscay ops (Instep patrols), over a beer in the Officers' Mess. The following afternoon (7th June), Joe and Geoff took off from Predannack on an Instep. They were leading a four-ship formation consisting of one of his 25 Squadron crews and two Australian crews from 456 Squadron, also detached, from their base at Middle Wallop, to support 264 Squadron. After a long, fruitless search for enemy aircraft, at around 1830hrs, smoke was sighted from a two-masted steam trawler travelling at about four knots, well beyond the normal distance from shore such vessels fished. The trawler, which bore the name Tadorne, was battened down, showing neither signs of life aboard, nor evidence of fishing gear. Joe ordered the formation to attack and records in his logbook:

ATTACKED TRAWLER 'TADORNE' ... WITH CANNON
& MG (320 CANNON, 1000 MG). 4 ATTACKS LEFT
IT SEVERELY DAMAGED AND SINKING.

So, after a very long Instep patrol of nearly 4.5 hours and more by luck than judgement, Joe had had a relatively benign introduction to the Battle of the Atlantic, the Bay of Biscay and Predannack. After four more days during which poor weather precluded further patrols, Joe and Geoff took off in the mid-afternoon of Friday 11th June for their second Instep Patrol.

This time, Joe is leading a formation of six aircraft – his three from 25 Squadron and three from 456 Squadron – flying in two Vics,[2] in loose line astern. Half an hour after take-off, one of the 456 Squadron aircraft reports engine trouble and returns to base. Reorganising the remaining five crews into one loose formation, Joe continues the patrol, flying between 50 and 100 ft over the sea. At about 1615 hrs, one of his wingmen reports sighting a formation of five Ju 88s high above them. Ordering them to close up in the climb, Joe manoeuvres his formation through scattered cloud, up-sun of the enemy aircraft. The Junkers indicate they have spotted the Mosquitos by starting a climb and firing three red star cartridges. At about 5,500 ft, Joe orders his formation to split and attack; he selects the rearmost Ju 88, which is closest to him. Three or four of the enemy aircraft then open fire on him from their dorsal gun turrets, but the tracers pass well over him. Whilst turning inside his quarry, Joe opens fire at full deflection[3] with a burst of less than one second. The enemy's port engine is seen to belch thick black smoke and he peels off to starboard in a dive. Following him closely, Joe gives him a second burst at about 300 yards' range. Sheets of flame are seen emanating from outboard of the Ju 88's port engine, but he is still ineffectually returning fire. Joe now closes to within 25 yards and delivers a three-second burst from dead astern, causing more flames to appear inboard of the port engine, quickly followed by thick black smoke from his starboard. This covers Joe's windscreen with oil, compelling him to peel off rapidly to starboard to avoid a collision.

Joe closes to within 25 yards and delivers a three-second burst. Still from actual gun camera footage. Singleton Private Collection.

Regaining some vision, Joe follows the Junkers into a steep dive and fires the fourth and final burst, whereupon pieces of the engine cowling and mainplane fly off. Joe and Geoff watch as two crewmembers of the Ju 88 bail out from the top hatch, one of who hits the tailplane. Their stricken aircraft rolls into a vertical dive and hits the sea, creating large, increasing, oil-streaked impact rings. This and his alarmingly close burst from 25 yards were graphically captured on Joe's gun camera, enabling him to readily claim a confirmed 'kill'. The crew of this Ju 88 – Fritz Hiebsch (Pilot), Peter Hoffman (Observer) and Erwin Seidel (Radio Operator) – were all killed.[4]

All the remaining enemy having now disappeared and, being short of fuel, Joe orders his scattered formation to return independently. During the engagement, Joe's formation claimed three other Ju 88s as 'Damaged'. After flights of over three hours, all his formation land safely. Joe's logbook entry reads:

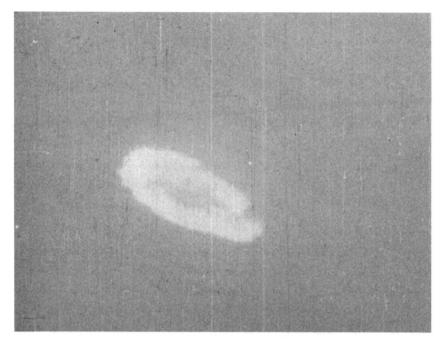

The end of the Ju88 and three crew members. Still from actual gun camera footage.
Singleton Private Collection.

MET 5 JU 88S AND ATTACKED – 1 JU 88 DESTROYED.

After landing and de-briefing, Joe learned that he is being recalled to Church Fenton. He is long overdue a rest from operations and he is to be replaced by his fellow 25 Squadron Flight Commander – Flight Lieutenant A. S. H. Baillie. Arriving at Predannack on Saturday 12th June, the same day Joe flew back to Church Fenton, Baillie teamed up with the two junior crews Joe left behind. He too is not afforded the luxury of a comfortable transition from night to day operations, or familiarisation with Bay of Biscay operations. Unlike Joe, however, he doesn't get the luck. On the day after he arrived – Sunday 13th June – four Mosquitos (three from 25 Squadron), led by Baillie, took off from Predannack. During the patrol, four Ju 88s were sighted and Baillie called the attack. On spotting their pursuers, the Germans broke formation and climbed into a layer of cloud. In the ensuing melee, Baillie completely lost sight and contact with both the enemy and his colleagues. Being at the end of an exceptionally long sortie he was very low on fuel so he returned to base and landed. The only sign of Baillie's missing formation was a radio call for an emergency homing to Predannack and a further message from one of the aircraft stating that they were being chased by the feared FW 190s. Not one of these three aircraft returned to base. The 25 Squadron Operations Record Book, a few days later, concluded eloquently:

> 'It would, however, seem that there is little hope of their survival, and the Squadron must necessarily face the loss of two very capable crews, and four officers for whom we hold a high regard'.

To lead a formation on an unfamiliar operation, within 24 hours of his arrival in an unfamiliar theatre, is a very high expectation indeed, both by Baillie himself and of him by his superiors. The effect on the man, of losing the six young aircrew in his formation, can only be guessed at. That he must have almost run out of fuel before he landed and faced the appalling reality, indicates that he was desperate not to abandon them. We can only guess what subsequent torment of 'survivors' guilt' Baillie went through. But it cannot be merely a tragic coincidence that exactly one year later, on 13th June 1944, Baillie and his navigator, flying a 25 Squadron Mosquito, went missing on an Intruder Operation, over enemy-occupied territory. He is buried near to where he died: in Brummen, in the Netherlands.

Joe Singleton's luck had held for now and he was to get a well-deserved break from front-line operations. But he would return and push his luck many more times yet, just as he had from the moment he walked into the RAF Recruiting Office in Leyland, Lancashire, with the outbreak of war imminent.

1.

From Paints to Pay Parades

(7th September 1939–9th June 1940)

Receiving Depot RAF Padgate

(7th September 1939–3rd November 1939)

Joe Singleton was 23 years old when he arrived at No. 3 Receiving Depot, Padgate, near Warrington, Lancashire, some 25 miles from his hometown of Leyland, on Thursday 7th September 1939. At the time he was manager of advertising and printing for the Leyland Paints and Varnish Co Ltd.

On that day, the *Daily Telegraph* reported that the first 'air raid' (actually no more than probing flights) on England had been repelled. Britain had declared war against Germany the previous Sunday (3rd September 1939) and the world was in a state of wholesale flux. Also on that day, Joe's local paper, the *Lancashire Telegraph*, replaced adverts on its front page for the first time, with news of the war.

Joe Singleton was born on 12th March 1916 in Prescot, on the eastern outskirts of Liverpool and now in Merseyside. His father, Abraham, came from local farming stock and was a mounted policeman. His mother, Mary Ellen (née Waterhouse) was a devout Catholic and had serious aspirations for Joseph, their only child, to become a priest. In furtherance of that ambition, his parents managed to get Joe into Fort Augustus Abbey School, staffed by Benedictine monks, on a Church Boy's grant for prospective Catholic priests. At what stage Joe chose paints and varnish over the cloth is unclear, but

Joe's first view of the RAF.

in 1939 Joe was volunteering to be a pilot. His motivation to do so could have been born of aviation-related events he experienced at his boarding school – on the southern edge of Loch Ness, Scotland, (today a holiday complex).

According to the school's history, a year or so after Joe arrived there in 1927, 'two graceful seaplanes moored by the school boathouse for the boys to inspect'. And, in the summer of 1932, at the start of his final year, a Gypsy Moth had landed, piloted by a Squadron Leader F. Noakes, who made three flights for the boys from a field south of the River Tarff.

In addition, he had 'fagged' for a senior boy – John Easton McFall – who had become a Flight Lieutenant in the RAF and who, six months before in March 1939, had been awarded the DFC[1] for bravery, as a reconnaissance pilot in Palestine during the Great Arab Revolt against British rule. He was not to know that McFall, shortly before he was killed in action in 1941, would be awarded a bar to his DFC whilst with 6 Squadron, Western Desert Air Force, flying a reconnaissance Lysander in Egypt during Rommel's offensive. Whatever Joe's motivation, he still had a long way to go before becoming an RAF pilot.

On 3rd September 1939, four days before his arrival at Padgate, the inaugural Aviation Candidate Selection Board had been convened for the first time at RAF Uxbridge in west London, to introduce objective testing procedures. Joe appears to have just missed this new regime. Instead, he would have undergone[2] the tried and tested pre-war selection procedure of the unstructured interview,

> *...entrusted to serving officers, who had no other brief than to find the right 'types'. They were expected, without guidance on the relative merits of personality, attainment and skills, and without the technical aids to measure them, to decide who should be accepted or rejected for aircrew selection. It was said later, that if a candidate had been to the 'right school', was tall, smart and in possession of rugby boots and a bible, he was officer material. If he rode horses as well, he was pilot material!* [3]

Joe had played rugby, hockey and cricket for the Abbey School first teams and been a senior prefect there; he had played hockey for the Leyland Co and was helping to create an athletics club for them, in addition to his current managerial position; he was also a scoutmaster at the St Mary's Leyland Troop. So, riding horses aside, Joe's interview appears to have gone went quite well... he was selected for training as a pilot and, as subsequent events bear out, probably earmarked as having officer potential.

Joe was sworn in – attested and enlisted as 967740 Aircraftman 2nd Class Aircrafthand Pilot Royal Air Force Volunteer Reserve on his first day. He was at Padgate for eight weeks. During this time, he was kitted out with an AC2 uniform ('hairies', in the vernacular), underwent numerous inoculations, attended lectures on a variety of basic subjects – Maths, English etc. – to confirm his school qualifications and spent many hours on the parade square drilling, stripping rifles, doubtlessly interspersed with plenty of bull. He would quickly have become aware that the RAF was in a state of fundamental turmoil and change. This had been brought about by a now massive expansion programme which had been instigated in 1935, albeit belatedly and, initially at least, half-heartedly. By 1939, the expansion was so far behind world events that crisis management was the order of the day. Nowhere was this more evident than in the flying training system Joe had just entered.

Between the wars, as with the other Services, the RAF was caught in the national dilemma. On the one hand, in the aftermath of WWI, there was the political (and civilian) bent to eschew war and militarism, leading to a tendency to underplay any threat to the nation and widespread sympathy towards pacifism. On the other hand, the military reality was that Nazi Germany was creating an ever-growing menace. The UK economic climate was generally dire and military spending was severely capped by the widely accepted 'ten year rule' – the assumption that the country would have a clear warning period of 10 years to the next war, within which rebuilding the military could and would be achieved in an orderly fashion. The RAF front line in 1934, when the politicians finally began releasing funds to the military in penny-packets, was a small fraction of the 1918 size and largely equipped with the same, or similar, aircraft types. Unsurprisingly therefore, new money was soaked up by modernisation and expansion of the front line. The paucity of training schools that did exist and the out-dated nature of their machinery (mostly vintage biplanes) were such that they could only hope to teach the fundamentals, to insufficient numbers. The gap between the schools' output standards, compared with that required by the new technology beginning to appear on front-line squadrons, inexorably grew. The stop-gap solution was that advanced training became less a primary activity for schools, more a secondary activity for the front-line squadrons. This was understandably hugely unpopular with these squadrons' aircrew, struggling to cope with the new technology designed to fight a sophisticated (potential) enemy. Far better, they thought, to practice escaping death against the Hun than risk it teaching 'sprogs'. As more and more new aircraft types were built and squadrons formed to meet the political imperative of the arms race with Germany, the need for more experienced pilots became intense. The result was instructors being taken away from the training organisation to feed the front line, just when their numbers needed boosting, further exacerbating the training gap:

The number of instructors available and the amount of training needed, together fixed the maximum rate at which expansion could go on efficiently. But at every stage of expansion, the actual rate set was well in excess of this maximum efficient rate. More instructors could not be found and so the standards of training had to suffer... The number of schools was kept down, and the fewest possible instructors taken from the front line, so that expansion would show the greatest possible number of squadrons, in the shortest time, for the money being spent.[4]

This problem was not resolved until 1944 – an ironic validation of the ten year rule.

RAF Feltwell

(3rd November 1939–5th December 1939)

Meanwhile, recruiting numbers, of which Joe in 1939 was one, were rocketing. The inevitable result was a huge backlog of students in the training system waiting for places on a course at the next stage. In 1939, at four weeks, the Receiving Depots' process was twice as long (presumably to mark time) as it would be only 18 months later. It was in this climate and, therefore little wonder that, on leaving Padgate, Joe held for another four weeks at RAF Feltwell in East Anglia, between Thetford and Downham Market, most likely engaged in menial or nugatory tasks.

He would have arrived at a newly built and opened (1937) 3 Group Bomber Command expansion airfield, home to 37 Squadron and their newly arrived Wellingtons and housed in Airmen's Barracks (if they had been built; if not in hastily erected huts, or even tents). Whilst there, Joe would have been well aware of the tension and excitement that accompanied 37 Squadron carrying out their first operational mission – a sweep of the North Sea against enemy shipping – on 15th November 1939.

Students arriving at ITW – this one a seaside hotel. Wikimedia Commons.

Initial Training Wing Cambridge

(5th December 1939–10th June 1940)

At the outbreak of war, it was recognised that far fewer holidays and degrees would be taken. The RAF exploited this by requisitioning university and holiday centres' facilities to satisfy the need for extensive new training intakes. Nos 1 and 2 Initial Training Wings were planned for Cambridge University and Nos 3, 4 and 5 were at the holiday resorts of St Leonards, Bexhill and Hastings respectively. It was a lottery as to whether your accommodation at ITW was a seaside hotel or undergraduates' rooms. Joe was allocated to No 1 ITW which opened at Cambridge on 27 September 1939, and was originally planned to take 1000 students but, in the event, started with only 800 'until the flying training organisation had expanded enough to require it. Even so there developed a long waiting period at ITWs before EFTS and … ITWs effectively became "holding pools".'[5]

Joe Singleton on right at ITW Cambridge. Singleton Private Collection.

The students were split amongst several campuses – amongst those used by the RAF were Trinity Hall, Jesus, St John's, Pembroke and Clare Colleges. The Commanding Officer of the ITW was a squadron leader who had the delicate job of establishing and operating his unit within the ivy-clad walls and keeping the peace with some very unwelcoming academic staff, who very much resented the intrusion. In one prickly exchange of letters, a professor remonstrates about the interruptions to his lectures due to the noise of the men being drilled. The Commanding Officer pacifies him by offering to get his men to mow the lawns and trim the hedges, which the professor grudgingly accepts.

ITW staff consisted of NCOs and education officers whose numbers steadily increased to teach more and more general education subjects, relevant or not, to fill in as course lengths became indefinite. Terence Kelly describes his experiences some six months after Joe:

ITW navigation lecture – Jesus College Cambridge. Note white flashes and belts.
Wikimedia Commons.

(there was) ... concentrated drilling and PT and learning radio telegraphy,
Morse-code (see photo of Joe), map-reading and plotting, how to strip a rifle and
such-like exercises ... I was one of 20 or so billeted in one of the colleges, where
quite a number of undergraduates were still in residence ... we held the rank
of AC2 and the pay was 2 shillings per day. We were, however, distinct from all
other non-commissioned personnel in that in our forage cap peaks we wore a piece
of white material ('white flash')[6] *which distinguished us from hoi polloi and of*
which we were immensely proud.[7]

There were also lectures on Law, Administration, Hygiene, Aircraft
Recognition and extensive pass/fail exams at the end of the course.
Another student remembers:

My first posting was to ITW at Cambridge where we were housed in College
accommodation as there was very little civilian activity in the University at that
time. We received our tuition in the college lecture rooms and our meals in the

dining rooms and were even allowed to use the college silverware. ITW headquarters was at Jesus!! We also did guard duties with rifles (no ammunition) at the Bridge of Sighs in the grounds of St. John's College and more than one professor had a near escape when he failed to respond to the command, 'Halt who goes there?'.[8]

During Joe's Cambridge experience much was happening in the outside world. Rationing was introduced in Britain early in the New Year but Western Europe was ominously quiet until the spring. The 'Winter War' between Russia and Finland concluded in March, and in the following month Germany invaded Denmark and Norway. Denmark surrendered almost immediately, but the Norwegians fought on until June, surrendering when British and French assistance was hastily withdrawn, due to German advances into Western Europe.

A Pay Parade for ITW students in the cloisters of St John's College Cambridge – for the 2/- per day. Note white flashes and belts. Wikimedia Commons.

AC Joe Singleton in 'Hairies'. Singleton Private Collection.

On 10th May – the same day that Winston Churchill replaced Neville Chamberlain as Prime Minister of the UK – Germany invaded France, Belgium and Holland, and Western Europe encountered the Blitzkrieg – or 'lightning war'. Germany's combination of fast armoured tanks on land, and superiority in the air, made a unified attacking force that was both innovative and effective. Despite greater numbers of air and army personnel – and the presence of the British Expeditionary Force – the Low Countries and France proved no match for the Wehrmacht and the Luftwaffe. Holland and Belgium fell by the end of May; Paris was taken two weeks later.

British troops retreated from the invaders in haste, and some 226,000 British and 110,000 French troops were rescued from the channel port of Dunkirk only by a ragged fleet, using craft that ranged from pleasure boats to Navy destroyers. The evacuation of Dunkirk was completed just four days before Joe left Cambridge to start his flying training; the stage was set for the Nazi invasion of Britain.

Churchill summed up the mood of the country:

> *This was a time when all Britain worked and strove to the utmost limit and was united as never before. Men and women toiled at lathes and machines in the factories till they fell exhausted on the floor and had to be dragged away and ordered home, while their places were occupied by newcomers ahead of time. The one desire of all the males and many women was to have a weapon … Nothing moves an Englishman so much as the threat of invasion, the reality unknown for a thousand years.[9]*

As Joe travelled from Cambridge to Hatfield he may have wondered about that mood, contrasting it with his last six months during which staff and students had been daily trying to find something useful to do, to fill the long wait for an EFTS slot. How dramatically things were about to change.

2.
Out of the Nest, into the Night
(10th June–31st October 1940)

No 1 Elementary Flying Training School – RAF Hatfield

(10th June 1940–24th July 1940)

Joe's arrival at Hatfield would have been a serious shock to the system. Geoffrey Wellum arriving at EFTS under similar circumstances describes his experiences:

> *The eventual arrival is not inspiring. A tremendous anti-climax ... As the transport deposits us at the main gate ... there is no one to meet us or tell us where to go or what to do (as they had at ITW). We just stand around in our shiny new uniforms (now AC1, white flashes), self-conscious and utterly lost. (Eventually) ... a fearsome individual ... a warrant officer or some such, forms us into threes and marches us to ... a lecture room of some sort, possibly the ground training block ... tells us to sit down and wait. After 20 minutes or so ... into the room strides a figure who has the look of authority. 'Attention, stand up when the Station Commander comes into the room!' a voice bellows ... so far we have only met two people and they both scare me stiff. God help us all!*

The Station Commander harangues the students for standing outside the main gate in a disorderly mob, and details what is expected of them under his command. They are dismissed some 40 minutes later and marched to the Officers' Mess. Wellum continues:

When things start to move next day, apprehensions are forgotten. A visit to stores, where I draw my flying kit. A new helmet with a facemask and a microphone in it, leather gloves and inners made of pure silk, overalls and a Sidcot[1] suit and flying boots. Down to the parachute section and then to the ground-training block. 'Take that pile of books and sign here.' Some pile it is too. The whole set-up reeks of hard work. My feet haven't touched the ground so far. It's been chase, chase, chase the whole damn time. It's going to be like school again with evening prep, examinations, the lot. That same afternoon I report to 2 Hangar.[2]

Joe's logbook entries for his first weeks on EFTS reveal an extraordinary intensity of effort. In 13 days, each interspersing flying and ground school lectures, Joe flies 24 sorties, totalling 11.5 hrs. Like Wellum, on the second afternoon of EFTS (11th June 1940), Joe is airborne on his first sortie in Tiger Moth N6874 with a Pilot Officer Forbes as instructor.

So Joe, having flown less than 12 hours, on 24th June 1940, flies his first solo, again in N6874. During that time, Joe has just one down day – Sunday 23rd June – it is unclear why. Poor weather? No aircraft? No instructor qualified to send him solo? Maybe even a rest day? For the remainder of month, he is flying four to six sorties per day many of them solo. He has one further down day – Saturday 29th June – and

No 5 War Course Hatfield (no2 Group). Joe fourth from left, rear rank. Singleton Private Collection.

by the end of June, just three weeks in to EFTS, he has started on the more applied skills of instrument flying and navigation.

Totals for Jun 40 (3 weeks):
48 sorties (33 Dual/15 Solo). 26.30 hrs (16.10 Dual/10.20 Solo)
Tiger Moth.

Tiger Moth DH.82 – No 10 EFTS RAF 1940. Image courtesy Clavework Graphics.

No matter how hectic that period was, on 17th June 1940, Joe would have learned that France had surrendered and maybe even heard Churchill's broadcast on the wireless in the mess or crew-room:

> *The news from France is very bad.. (but).. what has happened in France makes no difference to our actions and purpose. We have become the sole champions now in arms to defend the world cause. We shall do our best to be worthy of this high honour. We shall defend our Island home, and with the British Empire we shall fight on unconquerable until the curse of Hitler is lifted from the brows of mankind. We are sure that, in the end, all will come right.*

And on the 18th June:

> *Upon this battle depends the survival of Christian civilization.*
> *Upon it depends our own British life and the long continuity of our institutions, and our Empire. The whole fury and might of the enemy must very soon be turned on us.*

Hitler knows that he will have to break us in this Island, or lose the war. If we can stand up to him, all Europe may be free, and the life of the world may move forward into broad sunlit uplands.

But if we fail, then the whole world, including the United States, and all that we have known and cared for, will sink into the abyss of a new Dark Age, made more sinister and perhaps more prolonged by the lights of perverted science.

Let us therefore brace ourselves to our duty, and so bear ourselves that if the British Empire and commonwealth lasts for a thousand years, men will still say, 'This was their finest hour'.[3]

Spare a thought also for the instructors – the Pilot Officer Forbes of that world. The junior officer rank points to him being a 'creamed-off' Qualified Flying Instructors (QFI)[4] who, to get to be instructing at EFTS in 1940, would necessarily have joined the RAF before the war, maybe a year or so, perhaps via the Volunteer Reserve, for instance a University Air Squadron. He would have gone through elementary and advanced flying training, though probably with less backlog waiting than Joe was to experience. Just when he thought he might be destined for one of the new Hurricane squadron slots beginning to appear on the front line, he would be told he was going back into the training system to instruct the huge number of recruits now lining up at the RAF's door (the dilemma of preserving experience on the squadrons referred to above). The term 'creamed-off' was introduced with the aim of softening the blow; it is unlikely to have succeeded even if, as it usually was, accompanied by a 'guarantee' of a return to the front line for the next posting.

Each QFI would have had multiple students – four, five or six depending on his experience. Judging by Joe's flying rate there must have been excellent aircraft availability, so the instructors would be flying six plus sorties every day. To get maximum performance out of every student, each sortie (including solos) had to be briefed beforehand and debriefed afterwards (using chalkboards and model aircraft). Each sortie's details had to be entered in the authorisation sheets; each aircraft signed out and back in, via the Form 700, with precise take-off and land times; each instructional sortie written up, with assessments (sometimes lengthy and contentious) in the student's records. The physical effort alone is considerable: lugging parachutes in and out of aircraft; swinging airscrews when ground crew were not available (often); heaving on the control column (direct mechanical linkages to the control surfaces); resisting g-forces etc. The psychological strain of preventing a cack-handed student from killing you both, not to mention the huge gamble involved in sending a student off on his first, or indeed any, solo, should not be under-estimated. In between times, he would grab a sandwich and try to keep hydrated (it was summer). Instructors would be flying at two to three times the intensity of students who at least had the 'luxury' of a rest between sorties with a ground school lecture or three!

Pilot Officer Forbes took Joe through the entire EFTS syllabus (he rarely flew with a different instructor), except when taking 'RAF Tests' to check his progress. Joe completed the course on 22nd July 1940 with an assessment of 'Average', which was clearly deemed good enough for him to fly fighters.

Totals for No 1 EFTS RAF Hatfield (6 weeks):
87 sorties (52 dual/35 solo). 53.35hrs (27.15 dual/26.20 solo)
Tiger Moth.

The Battle of Britain had just started (10th July) and Dowding's Fighter Command, still licking its wounds from the Battle of France, was already desperately short of both aircraft and pilots. At this stage, Fighter Command deployed 52 squadrons, comprising 25 Hurricane, 19 Spitfire, 2 Defiant and 6 Blenheim squadrons which should have represented over 800 aircraft but, due to battle damage repair and unserviceabilities, only 644 were available for operations. To fully utilise these aircraft, over 1400 pilots were required, but only around 1200 were available. Though worse was yet to come, instructors and students alike would have been acutely aware of the urgency to fill Fighter Command's gaps.

No 3 Pre-Fighter Course – No 10 EFTS – RAF Yatesbury (Calne)

(24th July–10th August 1940)

In Wiltshire between Calne and Marlborough, Yatesbury was an early Royal Flying Corps (1912) grass airfield, used for civilian flying training between the wars, and requisitioned by the RAF in 1938. It was used for only a short time for RAF pilot training before becoming a flying school for wireless operators. Joe spent only two and a half weeks there, during which time he completed the first part of the Pre-Fighter course – an intensive advanced Tiger Moth syllabus – concentrating on instrument flying, navigation, spin recoveries, aerobatics, and it was here that he tasted formation and night flying for the first time. He is assessed again as 'Average'.

Totals for No. 3 Pre-Fighter Course – 10 EFTS – RAF Yatesbury (Calne): 29 sorties (14 dual/15 solo) 23.40 hrs (11.40 dual/12.0 solo) Tiger Moth

Harvard Conversion – No. 15 FTS – RAF Brize Norton

(10th–17th August 1940)

Joe's stay at Brize Norton was short and eventful. Arriving on Saturday 10th August, with his first sortie on the Monday, he will have had the weekend to unpack, settle in and start learning the checklist for a brand new aeroplane – the Harvard Mk 1 with a Pratt & Whitney Wasp engine. Geoffrey Wellum, a few months ahead of Joe in the process, related his experiences the day after his arrival at his Harvard station. His instructor tells him:

> 'This afternoon … we'll have a look at the Harvard aircraft and then tomorrow morning you will be on flying and we can really get down to it. Now the Harvard, as you know, is an American training aeroplane and … is a very modern and

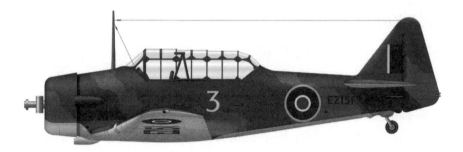

North American Harvard III – 352 Squadron RAF, 1944. Image courtesy
Clavework Graphics.

advanced aeroplane indeed. It has a retractable undercarriage and flaps and a constant-speed airscrew.' What on Earth's a constant-speed airscrew? '... you will find it a very pleasant and safe aeroplane to fly, but it is a low-wing monoplane with fairly high wing-loading and I must stress again that it must be treated with respect, especially at low speed. Pull it about like a Tiger Moth, abuse it, then it will turn around and bite you; understand?'

We reach a stubby, pugnacious looking aircraft in a hangar full of Harvards. It's a lot bigger than the little Tiger Moth, and I am conscious of this as I climb up on to the wing and lower myself into a fairly spacious cockpit. I find myself surrounded by so many dials, levers, switches, warning lights, taps and knobs that I just sit aghast: good grief! By the time we have finished, I feel saturated with facts and figures and absolutely punch drunk ... The Harvard has a rather bad name, having killed several experienced pilots ... (they) are what the RAF uses to sort the men out from the boys ... (The instructor) leaves me some typed notes on the fuel systems, hydraulics, engine data, revs and manifold pressure (whatever that is), settings to fly for climb, cruise, take-off and landing. 'You must memorise these ... and learn your cockpit and emergency procedures and drills off pat ... you must be able to find your way around the cockpit blindfolded.' ... Is the whole thing going to be too big for me? I feel alone and unsure. This Flying Training School, at the moment, is a remote and unfriendly place and I find the atmosphere depressing ... The next day we start in earnest. Parade is at 8 am ... on alternate days we fly in the morning and have ground work in the afternoon, and then vice versa.[5]

Joe's instructor is a Sergeant Kelly, who flies six dual sorties with him and sends him first solo on day five of the course – Friday 16th August 1940. That day at Brize Norton is notable for other reasons. Firstly, in the Battle of Britain, it marks the switch by the Luftwaffe from attacks

1940s aerial photograph of RAF Kidlington. Photo courtesy London Oxford Airport.

on radar installations (on the highly erroneous assumption that they were having no effect) to RAF airfields, against which 1700 sorties were flown that day. Secondly, in the evening around 1745 (presumably just as Joe was enjoying a well-deserved, celebratory first-solo beer at Happy Hour in the Mess), two Ju 88s stage a brilliantly audacious raid on Brize Norton, approaching with their wheels down as if they are Blenheims entering the circuit. Their bombs hit hangars full of fuelled-up aircraft. Forty-six Airspeed Oxfords (twin-engine training aircraft) and 11 Hurricanes at a maintenance unit on the airfield are destroyed; 7 other aircraft are also damaged, but no one is killed. A large number of airmen are called out to assist in the aftermath; there is no evidence Joe is one of them…

Intermediate Training School (Fighters) – RAF Kidlington

(17th August 1940–19th September 1940)

Whether connected to the bombing or not, all No.15 FTS Harvards left Brize Norton the following day (Saturday 17th August 1940) for RAF Kidlington, less than 30 miles away, north-west of Oxford, taking over 100 aircraft and all their school paraphernalia with them. Thus, Brize Norton represents where Joe converted to the Harvard. His resumption of instructional flying from Kidlington with Sergeant Kelly on Tuesday 20th August 1940, effectively marks the start of his Intermediate Flying Training Course. Requisitioned by the RAF in 1938 from Oxford City Council, Kidlington was a grass airfield with fewer amenities than those enjoyed by Brize Norton. Nevertheless, it grew rapidly and many of the hangars and administrative buildings built then, are still in use today.

On the day Joe started flying from Kidlington, he may have heard on the wireless, or read a transcript in the papers the following morning Churchill's words to parliament.

> *The gratitude of every home in our Island, in our Empire, and indeed throughout the world, except in the abodes of the guilty, goes out to the British airmen who, undaunted by odds, unwearied in their constant challenge of mortal danger, are turning the tide of war by their prowess and by their devotion.*
> *Never in the field of human conflict was so much owed by so many to so few.*[6]

With a prophetic reference to his own future war, which probably barely registered with Joe at the time, Churchill continued:

> *All our hearts go out to the fighter pilots, whose brilliant actions we see with our own eyes day after day, but we must never forget that all the time, night after night, month after month, our Bomber Squadrons travel far into Germany, find their targets in the darkness by the highest navigational skill, aim their attacks, often under the heaviest fire, often at serious loss, with deliberate careful precision, and inflict shattering blows upon the whole of the technical and war-making structure of the Nazi power.*

During August 1940, Joe moved stations twice and flew over 42 hours in two different aircraft types (Tiger Moth and Harvard). During the first half of September 1940, the remainder of his course is dominated by instrument flying (IF) tuition and navigational exercises, often with land-aways, including an unplanned one during an IF sortie with Sergeant Kelly on 16th September when his logbook entry is annotated:

**WEATHER THICK – LANDED ON FOOTBALL FIELD
ALDERSHOT CAMP THEN ON TO FARNBOROUGH
AND RETURN TO KIDLINGTON.**

Throughout ITS, he is again fortunate in having good instructor continuity, with Sergeant Kelly flying with him for almost all of the 29 dual sorties, aside from progress check sorties. Joe's logbook summary for the Intermediate phase of his training up to 18th September 1940 reads as follows:

Totals for Intermediate Training School – 15 FTS – 10 Aug 40–18 Sep 40 (RAF Brize Norton/RAF Kidlington): 52 sorties (23 dual/29 solo). 57.20 hrs (25.20 dual/32.00 solo).

At this stage he has accumulated a total of 136.10 total flying hours, including just 4.15 hours at night. As an indication of the intensity of life during his time at Kidlington (32 days), Joe had just four days when he did not fly – the weekend of 31 August–1st September, Sunday 15th and Tuesday 17th September. It is highly unlikely that this was all rest time and probable that at least a couple of those days were due to sickness, aircraft or instructor shortage.

Meanwhile, events in the outside world were momentous. Churchill summarises:

In the fighting between August 24th and September 6th the scales had tilted against Fighter Command. During these crucial days the Germans had continuously applied powerful forces against the airfields of south and south-east England. Their objective was to break down the day fighter defence of the capital, which they were impatient to attack. Far more important to us than the protection of London from terror bombing was the functioning and articulation of the airfields and the squadrons working from them. In the life-and-death struggle between the two Air Forces this was the decisive phase. There was much anxiety ... particularly at the headquarters of Fighter Command at Uxbridge ... If the enemy had persisted in the heavy attacks against [the airfields and sector stations] the whole intricate organisation of Fighter Command might have been broken down ... It was therefore with a sense of relief that the German attack turned on London on September 7th ... the enemy had changed his plans ... Goering should certainly have persevered against the airfields ... he made a foolish mistake. This same period ... had seriously drained the strength of Fighter Command as a whole. The Command had lost this fortnight 103 pilots killed and 128 seriously wounded, while 466 Spitfires and Hurricanes had been destroyed or seriously damaged. Out of a total [front-line] pilot strength of about a thousand, nearly a quarter had been lost. Their places could only be filled by 206 new, ardent, but inexperienced pilots drawn from training units, in many cases before their full courses were complete. The night attacks on London for ten days after September 7th ... were in effect for us a breathing space of which we had the utmost need. [7]

It was in this climate that, on 19th September 1940, Joe left Kidlington for Chipping Norton to begin his final phase of training.

Advanced Training School – No.15 FTS – RAF Chipping Norton/RAF Kidlington

(19th September 1940–31st October 1940)

On 20th September, Joe is presented with the coveted Flying Badge – he has got his 'Wings'. There is, however, a 10-day gap (18th– 28th September 1940) in Joe's logbook between ITS and ATS, the most likely cause of which is an enforced wait for the ATS to clear the backlog of students on the courses ahead of him. Despite the external pressures described above, it is possible that he was able to snatch some much-needed leave, in addition to yet another change of station. Chipping Norton was another grass airfield, smaller and with fewer facilities than even Kidlington. The accommodation was rudimentary, hastily erected wooden huts for accommodation and messing. Previously used as a relief landing ground, it is likely that the senior ATS students were detached there to relieve the pressure on Kidlington and it was considered they were now sufficiently experienced to cope with the challenges such a basic airfield would present. The airfield was returned to agricultural use in 1945. Today, aside from a few derelict shells of buildings there is little evidence of the frantic activities of 1940. Joe's logbook Record of Service shows that, at some stage during this period, the course moved back to Kidlington where they finished ATS, but it is incomplete in that it there is no date for when this occurred.

The advanced flying phase is characterised by much greater emphasis on self-reliance. There is very little dual tuition, and the luxury of continuity with the same instructor is removed. There is a great deal of solo flights and the course is introduced to 'mutual' sorties – two students flying together. During these, each student takes turns to act as safety pilot (annotated 'S.P.' in the logbook) keeping a lookout and map reading, while the other flies pre-calculated headings and timings around a route, on instruments under a hood. There continues to be a lot of routine navigation exercises but much more formation flying, including 'astern chases' to simulate dog fighting. In addition, there is a new discipline to be learned – the use of radios – both air-to-air within formations and taking/following instructions from ground controllers, anticipating working with sector controllers, which is a fighter squadron's bread-and-butter. Such is the shortage of advanced radios, most of which are consumed by the front line, that only a very few can be spared for training purposes. Of note, there is no night flying at all during this advanced phase, reflecting the modus operandi of the front-line up to that time, devoted to tackling Germany's primarily day-time attacks. Nevertheless, having switched their attention to attacking London, the Luftwaffe is now experiencing serious losses by day and, from the middle of September 1940, their emphasis begins to markedly shift towards night operations. The RAF is obliged to follow suit. The plain fact is, however, that defensive night fighting techniques and weaponry are very much in their infancy. With only six squadrons of Blenheims and Defiants to cover the role, it is not surprising that the training organisation had yet to recognise the need for night flying. Joe takes his final Flying Test from Kidlington with the Chief Flying

Instructor Squadron Leader Allen on 25th October 1940, passes and is again assessed as Average passing out of flying training.

Totals for Advanced Training School – 15 FTS – RAF Chipping Norton/RAF Kidlington (19 Sep–31 Oct 40).
48 sorties (10 dual, 23 solo, 15 mutual). 37.00 hrs (4.50 dual/ 32.10 solo & mutual).

Service Record Gap

(31st October 1940–3rd January 1941)

In tiny script in Joe's hand, tucked into the spine alongside his logbook entry for 30th August 1940 appear the letters 'L.F.'; an otherwise unremarkable solo sortie of 50 minutes in Harvard 7188 is recorded. It is this sortie, however, that is to fundamentally change the course of Joe's war. Whilst airborne that day, evidently with prior collusion, Joe meets up with two other students on the advanced course, also flying solo in their respective Harvards. They would all be aware that the next phase of their course would introduce them to the more advanced techniques including, excitingly, low flying. It seems that the three students had made a furtive pre-flight agreement to meet up and indulge in a foretaste of this low flying stuff. At their District Court-Martial on the 29th November 1940 they were each charged as follows:

> When on Active Service being the pilot of one of His Majesty's aircraft flying it at a height less than such height as was prescribed by a regulation issued under the authority of the Air Council in that he: in the vicinity of Moulsford, on the 30th August 1940, when pilot of His Majesty's aircraft Harvard N.7188, improperly and without permission flew the said aircraft over the land at an altitude of less than 2,000 feet contrary to the provisions of the King's Regulations and Air Council Instructions, paragraph 717, clause 7.

Moulsford is on the Thames just north of Goring. In his later years, Joe would relate, in a veiled-pride-wry-smile sort of way, whilst discussing the general topic of 'jankers' with his son, that he had himself spent a couple of months doing menial tasks, at the pleasure of the Station

Warrant Officer (jankers). It transpired that, having met up, the three miscreants spotted a dinghy sailing on the Thames (at Moulsford). One by one, they tried to demonstrate their real potential at low flying by seeing if the slipstream from their aircraft had an effect on the sails of the dinghy, better yet if they could blow it over.... It was somewhat unfortunate that the said dinghy happened to be in eyeshot of an RAF Group Captain, presumably enjoying a little respite from the war, doing a spot of fishing. Equally unfortunate was the Group Captain's ability to record the tail numbers of the three offending aircraft and track down their origins. 'L.F.' was Joe's cipher for 'Low Flying', although it is not known whether he put it there before or after the inevitable summons, hat on, to the Flight Commander's office. 'Now, about your solo on the 30th of August, Singleton...'

So Joe completed the final two months of his Advanced Training School under the shadow of an impending Court-Martial. It does not seem to have to have had a significant effect on his performance; he graduated from ATS and was ready for the next step.

In the event, the verdict of the Court was, of course, guilty and he was sentenced to a loss of seniority of 28 days (29th November–26th December 1940). Such high jinks, whilst senior students are airborne solo at the same time, was by no means uncommon, then or since. Especially at that critical moment in the war, many would have advocated turning a blind eye, on the grounds that such bravado is exactly what was needed from putative fighter pilots. Clearly, an external senior officer lodging an official complaint ruled out such an approach. The rules had been transgressed and, war or no war, the legal process had to be followed. The light sentence was a reflection of the Court's view of the gravity of the offence. But, most significantly, the episode resulted in Joe disappearing from the scene for two months – on 'jankers' – until the outcome of the Court-Martial was known and his future decided.

Joe's expectation in October 1940 would surely have been that he would form part of the replenishment of the seriously depleted Spitfire and Hurricane day fighters. His delayed promotion from LAC to Sergeant came on 22nd December 1940. By the time he returned to flying in the New Year of 1941, the need to mount an effective defence against the Night Blitz, now in full swing, was paramount. The day-fighter squadrons' manning problems were diminishing with the number of Luftwaffe daylight raids.

By the end of 1940, German air raids had killed 15,000 British civilians. One of the worst attacks occurred on the night of 14th–15th November against Coventry, when 449 Luftwaffe bombers destroyed 50,000 buildings in a firestorm, killing 568 people and injuring many more. Public and political opinion was outraged. The RAF's woefully inadequate night defence capability now had become the major deficiency to be addressed. The shortage of instructors in the training organisation was as critical as ever; little wonder, therefore, that Joe was to be 'creamed off' to instruct in the nascent night fighter world.

3.
Creamed Off
(3rd January 1941–October 1941)

No 54 Operational Training Unit – RAF Church Fenton

(3rd January 1941–17th June 1941)

Joe records his arrival at Church Fenton as 3rd January 1941, whilst his first logbook sortie entry is 26th January. With two new (to him) aircraft types appearing very shortly thereafter, it is likely that he spent those 3 weeks in ground school and trainers, aimed at both aircraft conversion and instructional techniques. No 54 OTU was a night fighter training establishment, taking pilots through dual instruction on the Tiger Moth and the Miles Master to the single pilot cockpit (with a turret gunner) of the Boulton Paul Defiant.

Night Fighter Development

Night fighting had inevitably been the poor relation in the development of all types of defensive air operations. Before the winter of 1940, no enemy aircraft had the capability of operating effectively (i.e. dropping bombs with any accuracy) in cloud, at night or both. Blind flying instruments alone were at best rudimentary; accurate navigation, target location and identification were major shortcomings. The creation of the Chain Home (CH) radar system and the revolutionary command

and control system of Fighter Command had been fundamental to winning the Battle of Britain by day. However, the Luftwaffe had by now found the way to harness similar technology to enable them to switch their operations to significant effect, initiating the night Blitz on London and Britain's industrial centres. Their radars and radio navigational aids enabled them to get to and drop their bombs on large targets, despite stringent blackout measures. Once again the RAF was in catch-up mode – finding cities to bomb at night was one thing, finding the aircraft attacking them, entirely another.

> *The CH system had rather coarse limitations in discrimination and plotting accuracy. It was ideal for giving early warning of hostile aircraft, and for giving their present and likely future position accurately enough for defending fighters to be vectored by ground controllers to within five miles and, with luck, to within two or three miles and within about a mile (say 5,000 ft) of the same height. By day this was good enough; there was never to be a single occasion in the Battle of Britain when RAF fighters were to be vectored on to the enemy and not see him. But at night a miss was as good as a mile. Knowing the enemy – not a formation at night but a single bomber – was within five miles and possibly two, was merely frustrating. The night fighter had no means of knowing in which direction to search, and experience was to show that a skilled and experienced pilot could spend an hour within five miles of a known enemy aircraft, and even accompany it on its bombing run across the target, see its bombs explode, and still [have no idea where the bomber was, let alone see it].*[1]

Searchlight and anti-aircraft gun operators suffered in the same way. The answer to the problem had been recognised in some quarters several years before – put a radar and receiver on the defending aircraft, to conduct the final, detailed hunt and attack, independently of ground stations. This solution, however, involved the generation of radio pulses of much shorter wavelength than that generated by CH radars; this necessitated more power. The CH system used enormous amounts of electricity drawn from the national grid; their aerial arrays covered acres. Generators capable of producing even more power were feasible but, at that stage were so large that there was no hope of them fitting into the largest aircraft in the RAF inventory, let alone fighters, which were small single-seat aircraft, tightly packed with armaments and fuel. The technological battle of developing airborne interceptor (AI) radars by miniaturisation continued apace. But, needless to say, the stress on the aircraft manufacturers to satisfy the massive demand for day fighters meant little or no attention being paid to developing a night fighter platform, to carry whatever would be the result of the AI research.

> *By sheer luck, two aircraft companies chose to build such machines in the absence of any official interest, not appreciating quite how useful their products would turn out.*[2]

More of which later, in the meantime, night fighting was a case of making do with what was actually to hand – enter the Defiant.

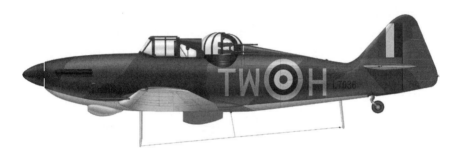

Boulton-Paul Defiant Mk I - 141 Squadron RAF 1940. Image courtesy Clavework Graphics.

Boulton Paul Defiant – Specifications

Powerplant:	One 1,030 hp Rolls-Royce Merlin III twelve-cylinder liquid cooled engine.
Span:	39 ft 4 in (11.99m)
Length:	35 ft 4 in (10.77m)
Max Speed:	304 mph (490 km/h) at 17,000 ft (5,181 m)
Armament:	Four .303in Browning machine guns mounted in electrically operated turret.
Accommodation:	Pilot and air gunner.

Recognition: Most prominent feature from the side is the gun turret, mounted immediately behind the pilot's cockpit. Large, triangular tail. From below, thick, straight wings, with the outer section swept forward, house the wide main undercarriage.

The concept of a gun turret-armed defensive fighter emerged in 1935, at a time when the RAF anticipated having to defend Great Britain against massed formations of unescorted enemy bombers. The RAF believed that its turret-armed bombers, such as the Vickers Wellington, would be able to penetrate enemy airspace and defend themselves without fighter escort and that the Luftwaffe would be able to do the same. The delays in production, which resulted in only three Defiants being delivered before the outbreak of war, meant that it could not be used in 1940 in its originally planned role – that of standing defensive patrols. The long period that passed, between the first conception of the Defiant turret fighter and its operational acceptance, impaired its usefulness. The first unit to equip with the type was No. 264 Squadron,

Formation of 264 Squadron Defiants.

which moved to Martlesham Heath to take delivery in December 1939. Engine and hydraulic malfunctions caused a grounding order late in January 1940, which was lifted the following month.

In the early stages of the war, during the expeditionary phase in France including the evacuation of Dunkirk, the Defiant operated as a daylight interceptor, alongside the hard-pressed Hurricanes and the few Spitfires then available. Initially they enjoyed a reasonable degree of success. They were often mistaken for Hurricanes, which the Luftwaffe knew had forward firing guns and therefore attacked from the rear quadrants, only to be surprised that they were flying into the Defiant's most lethal arc of gunfire. Against bombers, the Defiant's extremely heavy turret armament was very effective; and by operating mixed formations of Defiants and Hurricanes the RAF could make use of the superficial resemblance between the two types to confuse and trap German fighters. However, if a Messerschmitt caught a Defiant on its own, they began inflicting appalling casualties. The technique of the Defiant pilot, positioning his aircraft with the gunner's field of fire in mind, was feasible against slow bombers but quite impossible in a fast dogfight. In addition, since the Defiant turret could not fire directly forwards and avoid its own cockpit or propellers, it did not take long for the Luftwaffe to discover that Defiants were highly vulnerable to head-on attacks. That, coupled with the reduced performance due to the aerodynamics of the turret and that, in an emergency, a Defiant gunner had very little chance of escaping from his turret, resulted in losses in the Defiant squadrons – primarily Nos 264 and 141 Squadrons – mounting so alarmingly that their withdrawal from the day front line became the only feasible option.

Boulton Paul Defiant – Night Fighter Evolution

In theory, turret-armed fighter pilots would approach an enemy bomber from below or from the side, in order that their gunners could coordinate their fire. This separation of the tasks of flying the aircraft and firing the guns, it was thought, would allow the pilot to

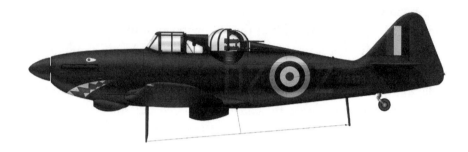

Boulton Paul De ant NFMk1 No.151 Squadron RAF. Image courtesy Clavework Graphics.

concentrate on the inherent problems of night flying and putting the fighter into the best position for the gunner to engage the enemy.

With only the limited assistance from CH radars available at night, however, clearly the bulk of the burden of locating, tracking and positioning the enemy still fell to the aircrew. On leaving FTS, Flying Officer James Ghilles Benson relates:

I left there on July 25th [1940] and reported to 141 [Defiant] Squadron, where I was told I was replacement for eleven pilots [and, presumably air gunners] who had been shot down the previous week ... Because the squadron had few aircraft and fewer pilots, it was retired to Grangemouth to re-equip ... (later) it had been decided that the squadron would probably go on to night fighting, we moved to the Edinburgh area to do some night-flying training, which was sadly lacking at that time ... the meagre facilities available for night flying ... It seems strange to realise the fantastic difficulties put in the path of anybody trying to operate in an aircraft at night. We were flying from grass airfields with no runways. The maximum number of lights allowed at first was six 'glim' lights which certainly showed only a glimmer of light. These were the only lights available for both take-off and landing. There was little or no help to be had from Flight [Air Traffic] Control, and this, coupled with the fact that at the time we had very poor radios which were all too liable to pack up, made life and training in general fairly exciting ... I will always remember my first night patrol from Biggin Hill [Oct 40]. I took off with the aid of six glim lamps, which were immediately extinguished as I went into the air [as a blackout measure]. I was shot at by the airfield defences as I took off, coned by searchlights soon after and then got lost in cloud, only to find my radio had packed up! I was told that if I was lost I should look for a blue searchlight. Never having seen a searchlight from the air before, I found that they all looked blue as I approached them. To my horror, however, each time I tried to get a homing from one of them, I was coned or followed around [i.e. being tracked by AA batteries]. I decided it would be safer in cloud, despite ... being completely lost ... [We discovered later that] we had the distinguished experience of flying right through the London balloon barrage, which we fortunately did not see. We then sighted an enemy aircraft which we chased but lost in cloud. We were only rescued from the necessity of having to bail out [through lack of fuel] by the action of a brave man at Gatwick Airport. He turned on the flashing beacon in the middle of an air raid, thereby enabling us to do a rather dicey landing there.[3]

Despite this graphic illustration of the shambolic state of night fighting, it was a fact that, in the winter of 40–41, Defiants scored more kills at night (though still precious few) than all the Spitfires and Hurricanes put together. This explains why, when Joe arrived on 54 OTU, the Defiant was regarded as the best night fighter the RAF had and so much effort was being put into training, to improve both men and machine. The obvious and immediate drawback was that the Defiant had a single pilot cockpit making dual instruction impossible. To overcome this, the OTU was equipped with a two-seat trainer closest to the Defiant in terms of size, performance and handling – the Miles Master. The Tiger Moth was used as an introduction to the advanced night operating techniques, building on those covered at the ATS, needed for both the Master and the Defiant. Having graduated from the ATS for fighters (albeit three months previously) it was clearly considered that Joe did not need to undergo the niceties of the Tiger Moth. So it was that on 26th January 1941, he flew one dual sortie with a Pilot Officer Robertson, his first in a Master, immediately followed by two solo sorties. Welcome back, Singleton.

Having re-acquainted himself with the Tiger Moth and having been checked out on the Master by day and night, on 10th February 1941 Joe flew the Defiant for the first time. For this and for the first few Defiant sorties he flew solo, without a gun operator, getting to know the local area by day, practicing use of the Defiant's radio and oxygen system.

Miles Master – Evolution

In January 1939 large extensions to the Miles factory were completed and opened by the Secretary of State for Air. These were necessary to cope with a large contract for the Master I high-speed advanced training monoplane: a two-seater powered by a 536 kW Rolls-Royce Kestrel 30 engine. Nine hundred were built.

Soon after the outbreak of World War II, the prototype Master II flew for the first time. It was based on the Master I but powered by a 648 kW Bristol Mercury XX radial engine. Production amounted to approximately 1,800 aircraft, a number of which were sent to South Africa. Master IIs were also acquired by the air forces of Egypt, Portugal and Turkey. One Master II was used in connection with rocket experiments.

The Master III was a further development of the Master series, powered by a 615 kW Pratt & Whitney R-1535-SB4G Wasp Junior radial engine. A total of 602 were built. Maximum level speed was 372 km/h.

Miles M9A Master I advanced trainer.

M.19 Master Mk II Specifications

Model	M.19 Master Mk II	
Engine	1 x Bristol Mercury XX, 649kW	
Weights		
Take-off weight	2,528 kg	5,573 lb
Empty weight	1,947 kg	4,292 lb
Dimensions		
Wingspan	11.89 m	39 ft 0 in
Length	8.99 m	30 ft 6 in
Height	2.82 m	9 ft 3 in
Wing area	21.83 m²	234.98 ft²
Performance		
Max. speed	389 km/h	242 mph
Ceiling	7650 m	25,100 ft
Range	632 km	393 miles

Joe's first night sortie is on 24th February in a Defiant and the next day he flies twice with gun operators practicing air firing. For all of March, he gets a thorough knowledge of the aircraft and its modus operandi: working on interceptions with ground radio and radar controllers; instruments take-offs (to ensure being able to get airborne with little or no visibility); and positioning his gunner for air firing practice. The intensity of this work-up is illustrated by the logbook entry for 21st March – a night search and homing (radar), with R/T homing, exercise with a Sgt Gaunt in the rear – to which is appended the laconic comment in red ink:

LOST WING TIP ON HILL NEAR ILKLEY – GOT BACK OK

He also records 30 minutes flying in cloud. A reasonable assumption, therefore, is that, at some stage during the homing and positioning to attack the 'enemy' – most likely another Defiant – he became disorientated and only just managed to recover the aircraft in time.

Indeed, many more night fighter crews met their deaths in this way, rather than at the hands of the Luftwaffe.

Interspersed with the Defiant sorties in March, he continues to develop his instructional techniques on the Master, including mutual sorties (with another trainee instructor) practising back-seat landings so that, were a pupil (who sat in the front seat of the Master) to mess up an approach, he would be able to take over and land safely.

**Totals for Jan–Mar 41 (Conversion to Night Fighter Instructor): 50 sorties (36 Day/15 Night), 51.45 hrs.
Day: Tiger Moth – .50, Master – 8.30, Defiant – 19.35.
Night: Tiger Moth – 3.15, Master – 2.05, Defiant – 14.25.**

Having now acquired a full understanding of what his students needed to know about the Defiant, on 5th April 1941, Joe begins full-time instructing on, mainly, the Master and the intensity of life – flying up to nine sorties per day, an arduous regimen previously described for instructors during Joe's own training, begins.

During April 1941, he flies 51 sorties, 37 of them instructing on the Tiger Moth (8) and Master (29), mostly by day. In addition, he flies 13 sorties in the Defiant, not just to keep his hand in. On the 24th, having already flown four day and one night sorties in the Master, he takes off on his first recorded operational sortie in a Defiant. A tone of distinct anti-climax is struck in the logbook entry:

*VECTORED ON TO BANDIT OVER YORK – NO RESULTS –
RETURNED TO BASE AFTER OBSERVER CORPS LOST BANDIT
& SO UNABLE TO OBTAIN FURTHER PLOTS.*

What this reveals is that 54 OTU instructors were, in effect, moonlighting from their day jobs and, as part of the network of fighter units defending the northern industrial centres, were flying operational night sorties, when the instructing day/night was over. It also reveals that the system was sufficiently advanced to be operating with radar units, getting vectors by radio, despite the poor performance of CH radars inland. Finally, it also shows that he placed what seems, at this distance, an odd degree of faith in the Observer Corps' ability to track bandits at night. Like the Defiant aircrew, all they had to penetrate the dark, by and large, were their own eyes and ears. Most likely, at this stage, Joe was completely absorbed with his own difficulties of operating in this environment and was unaware of others'. Later on, it would become common practice for night fighter squadrons to pay regular liaison visits with radar, searchlight and Observer Corp units to discuss and understand each other's problems.

On 28th April, Joe records his second operational sortie, adding:

SCRAMBLE TO 10,000FT OVER BASE – NIL DOING.

It must have been frustrating to have the limitations of the weapon system on which he was instructing so starkly exposed. A curious anomaly appears on 23rd April when Joe spends 40 minutes doing circuits and landings in a twin-engined Airspeed Oxford – used to train pilots for multi-engined aircraft – perhaps the beginnings of the realisation that the much-needed and anticipated airborne AI would have to be fitted in an aircraft larger than the Defiant?

The Night Blitz reached its zenith on 10th–11th May with heavy bombing of London. On 54 OTU, May 1941 followed a similar pattern to April: instructional sorties in the Master, mostly by day, interspersed with Defiant sorties – air tests and formation practice by day. There are two operational sorties: the first a night scramble on 2nd May, clearly drawing another blank (*SCRAMBLE OVER BASE – PATROLLED AT 7000FT*); the second on May 18th, interestingly, a day scramble. One presumes and hopes that the fighter controllers who scrambled Joe were not only short of regular day fighters but also comfortable that the 'bogey' – an unidentified radar blip – was a bomber, unescorted by German fighters known to be lethal to Defiants. In any event, the logbook entry further illustrates the uncertainties that still dogged the ground radar operators. It reads:

Royal Air Force Airspeed AS.10 Oxford II. Photo courtesy Bob Brown.

SCRAMBLE TO FIND BOGEY WHICH WAS FLYING AT 11,000FT 40 MILES SOUTH – TURNED OUT TO BE A MANCHESTER![4]

There is another possible explanation: Joe was promoted, commissioned as a Pilot Officer on 17th May, an event which almost certainly sparked a good deal of merriment in the Mess the previous night – and sore heads the next day...

Another unexplained peculiarity also occurred on 20th and 21st May when Joe records another first by captaining a Fairey Battle, each time with the same two airmen passengers. The first sortie logged as 'LOCAL FLYING PRACTICE' the second as 'TO CATFOSS FOR A/F – WEATHER U/S' (A/F = air firing?, u/s = unserviceable). The Battle, a light bomber carrying a navigator and gunner, in tandem behind the pilot, was another failed experiment from pre-war designs, now used for training. Since Catfoss (near Bridlington) had target-towing aircraft and an offshore firing range, it is a fair guess that Joe was acting as cab-driver for the gunner at the back to get in some shooting practice with the single machine gun fitted to the Battle – but the weather (probably low cloud or poor visibility) precluded it. The only other Battle sorties in Joe's logbook appear the following month. On 12th June, he flies two return journeys to Catfoss, each time picking up two passengers with no other activities recorded. Equally inexplicable is Joe's ferrying a Battle, flying alone, from Shawbury (Salop) to East Fortune (East of Edinburgh) on 24th June.

Joe makes no flights in the Tiger Moth in May 1941, which marks the hiatus between the phasing out of the Moth and introducing the Miles Magister, in mid-June, as 54 OTU's basic training machine – as a low wing monoplane, rather more closely resembling the Master and Defiant.

June 1941 follows the same routine of tuition, with Joe making his final operational sortie in the Defiant on 14th June simply described as '*NIGHT OPERATIONAL PATROL*', proving to be as fruitless as the previous four.

A rationalisation of the force on 17th June, leads to Joe being transferred, along with all the Defiants, to No 60 OTU at East Fortune. 54 OTU remained at Church Fenton and, soon thereafter began re-equipping with Blenheims, recently withdrawn from the front line, and to be used as lead-in to the next big thing in night fighters – the Beaufighter. The Beaufighter was proving to be one of the platforms, which, by the 'sheer luck' referred to by Bill Gunston, was proving suitable, in terms of both size and performance, for the latest output from the boffins creating airborne radars for AI. The writing was on the wall for the Defiant as a night fighter, because it simply did not have the space to fit the new equipment. Knowing only too well the deficiencies of the Defiant and almost certainly being aware of the potential of AI, Joe probably recognised that East Fortune represented a further step away from the action both geographically and, for a fighter pilot yearning for the latest technology, in terms of aircraft type. Nevertheless, he would perhaps have been comforted by the knowledge that he was over halfway through his stint as an instructor – nine or ten months was the usual tour length – and he could be sure of a front-line posting after that. After all, that's what 'creamies' were promised, wasn't it?

RAF No. 218 Squadron Fairey Battles over France, c. 1940.

No 60 OTU – RAF East Fortune

(17 June–3 November 1941)

Joe's time at East Fortune began eventfully enough. On 19th June, two days after arriving (and only five since his last trip out of Church Fenton), he flew the Magister for the first time (by day). The next day (20th) he flew a day dual instructional sortie, followed by a series of night sorties with students on the fourth of which he made an emergency landing, recorded as:

> **FORCED LANDING, SUCCESSFULLY IN FIELD**
> **(ENGINE CUT ON TAKE OFF).**

An engine failure after take-off, with insufficient height to turn back to the airfield leaves the pilot with no time to do anything more than push the nose rapidly down (to maintain flying speed) and head for the nearest suitable field, within a narrow arc in front of the aircraft

Miles Magister. Photo courtesy Alan Wilson.

(large turns invite stalling). The pilot will normally have pre-selected the field, in his mind, for that particular runway from experience of previous take-offs. If wise, he would have practiced it a few times, by closing the throttle and having a good look at fields within gliding range, checking for ditches, before climbing away. At night, the most he can do, is to concentrate on gliding the aircraft into the black hole and wait for the ground to meet the fixed undercarriage, hoping for the best. Joe had flown from East Fortune for less than an hour in daylight when faced with this nasty situation; he was blessed with the skill and luck needed to walk away unscathed.

Though continuing to be very busy, the remainder of Joe's time on 60 OTU is relatively uneventful with the exception of another engine failure in a Magister, this time by day, whilst returning from St Athan in South Wales to East Fortune. The matter-of-fact (not in red ink) entry reads:

FORCED LANDING IN FIELD NEAR BURTON ON TRENT DUE TO ENGINE FAILURE. NO DAMAGE.

Amongst all the Magister and Master tuition, plenty of Defiant sorties are flown, including some army co-operation sorties, air to ground firing practice and a lot of formation. No doubt due to the relatively remote location and Germany's focus shifting more to the east around this time,[5] there are no further scrambles or live operational missions. There is a marked reduction in night flying once the Defiants have relocated to East Fortune. This, coupled with what appears to be an exploration of its utilisation for Army co-operation, may be an indication that there is a general recognition that the Defiant is no longer the platform of choice as a night fighter. At the end of October 1941, Joe is rated as 'Exceptional' (the highest possible assessment) as a night fighter instructor, and finally heads towards the front line, and away from single-engine aircraft.

Totals for Apr–Oct 41 (Night Fighter Instructor): 261 sorties (239 Day/42 Night), 252.05 hrs.
Day: Tiger Moth – 5.15, Magister – 37.45, Master – 110.35, Defiant – 40.05.
Night: Magister – 37.45, Master – 31.30, Defiant – 5.05.

Just over two years after joining the RAF, Pilot Officer Singleton fulfils his ambition and takes his position on the front line, as a pilot on 25 Squadron.

4.

Front Line at Last – Where's the Action?

(3rd November 1941–16th May 1942)

No 25 Squadron, RAF Wittering

(3rd November 1941–25th January 1942)

25 Squadron had been at Wittering for a year when Joe arrived there on 3rd November 1941. By chance, a 25 Squadron photograph had been arranged for the following day. The newness of his surroundings may have something to do with him looking the least relaxed of the front row of aircrew (see page 45: Joe is fifth from left).

25 Squadron had moved to Wittering a year earlier, from airfields in the south east (Debden, North Weald, Martlesham Heath), where its role during the Battle of Britain had been that of night defence of London with the Blenheim. As already described, with little night trade during that time and with minimal capability, the squadron could contribute little to that Battle. Indeed, its unfortunate claim to fame, up until then, was that two of its Blenheims were mistakenly shot

down by a Hurricane patrol on 3rd September 1940. A New Zealander – Flying Officer M. J. Herrick holds the distinction of recording the first WWII kill for the squadron, in a Blenheim, when he shot down two Heinkel 111s on 4th September 1940. The squadron began re-equipping with Beaufighters in the same month and immediately got to work trialling whatever rudimentary AI equipment the boffins were working on at the time. The first 25 Squadron Beaufighter kill came on 15th November 1940. In 1941, the squadron destroyed six in May and seven in June, mainly over the Midlands and East Anglia, apart from reports of 'damaged' and 'probable' kills. After that, the incidence of raids dropped sharply (in line with the Luftwaffe's switch to the Eastern Front and Joe's own experience at East Fortune).

With the arrival in late 1940 of 25 Squadron (with Blenheims and Beaufighters) and 151 Squadron (with Defiants and Hurricanes), Wittering became a specialist night fighter station at the forefront of experimenting with the various new night fighting techniques.

These included trying different camouflage paints when it was discovered, counterintuitively, that a black paint scheme rendered the aircraft more visible, as a dark shadow against a usually less than black night sky. After much trial and error, the paint scheme eventually settled on was dirty white on the leading edges with the rest of the airframe a blue-grey colour. Despite widespread reservations, this paint scheme was adopted throughout the night fighter force. Meanwhile, 151 Squadron became a test-bed for rather more (with hindsight) oddball techniques to overcome the see-in-the-dark conundrum: turbinlites and flare burning. 'Turbinlite' operations involved a specially adapted aircraft, whose guns had been replaced by a very powerful searchlight. The Turbinlite aircraft, closely accompanied by two Hurricanes, would be homed onto an attacker by Ground Controlled Interception (GCI). On sighting the enemy, the Turbinlite would manoeuvre into a position where he could switch on his searchlight, so that the Hurricanes could carry out the attack. 'Flare burning' worked on a similar principle but involved, as the name implies, illuminating the target for the Hurricanes by dropping flares at precisely the right time and place.

NO. 25 SQUADRON. NOVEMBER 4TH. 1941.

Sgt. Risner.   Sgt. Felton.   Sgt. Holloway.   Sgt. Harper.   Sgt. Sheffield.   Sgt. Silvester.   F/Sgt. Thomas.   Sgt. Sheod.   Sgt. Spence.

Sgt. Keith.   F/Sgt. Holloway.   Sgt. Hill.   Sgt. Holtwell.   Sgt. Hollis.   Sgt. Bennett.   Sgt. Johnson.   Sgt. Bradshaw.   Sgt. Pound.   F/Sgt. Curtis.   Sgt. Scope.

P/Off   F/Off   P/Off   P/Lient,   S/Ldr.   W/Cmdr.   W/Cmdr.   S/Ldr.   F/Lieut.   F/Off   P/Off   P/Off
Sellick   Pickustt.   Singleton.   Stoneman, B.E.M.   Wray.   Plennanox, D.F.C.   D. F. W. Alchedvy, D.F.C.   Clayton, D.F.C.   Arington, A.F.C.   Shaw.   Britani.   Chote.
                            (Engineer)

P/Off   F/Lieut   P/Off   P/Off
Camb-Miller   Waddington.   Chote.   Cooke.
(Intelligence)

P/Off   P/Off
Sandford   Anderson
                                                                                                                                                                              (Adjutant)

25 Squadron 4 November 1941. Singleton Private Collection.

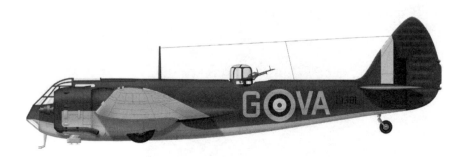

Bristol Blenheim Mk.I 84 Squadron RAF, 1941. Image courtesy Clavework Graphics.

Bristol Blenheim cockpit. Photo courtesy Mike Murphy.

Both techniques were every bit as clumsy and complicated as they seem, prone to accidents and yielding little success. It is a measure of just how desperate the RAF was to try anything that might work, before AI proved itself worthy. Turbinlite aircraft, in particular were persevered with for a surprisingly long time (well into 1943), primarily because they were useful as platforms for developing early AI prototypes.

So Joe arrived at Wittering with the squadron in a steady routine of non-operational night flying, leading to plenty of practice interceptions of

Bristol Beaufighter Mk.IF 25 Squadron RAF, 1940. Image courtesy Clavework Graphics.

friendly targets, but with few enemy contacts and even fewer engagements. Although, technically, still on 54 OTU until 3rd November, Joe's first 25 Squadron sortie is on 2nd November with his 'B' Flight Commander – Squadron Leader W. J. Alington[1] in a Beaufighter out of Wittering, designed to familiarise him with the squadron's aircraft, before he goes off on his twin-engine conversion course.

RAF Catfoss – Twin-Engine Conversion Course

(18th November–4th December 1941)

Situated four miles west of Hornsea on the Yorkshire coast, Catfoss was home to No. 2 (Coastal) Operational Training Unit and operated from three grass runways at this time, around a year before concrete runways were laid. Although parented by Coastal Command and primarily a unit for training their long-range maritime aircraft crews, it also trained Fighter Command pilots on Blenheims when converting them from single- to twin-engined aircraft.

The Blenheim was developed by the Bristol Aeroplane Company before the war from a small, fast (for then) 6–8-seater passenger aircraft[2] into a light bomber. Before it saw service as a bomber, however, it was recognised as being too vulnerable to Luftwaffe fighters, and its utility as a long-range fighter was investigated. Like the Defiant, its limitations and consequent losses in daylight were manifest, leading to its 'relegation' to night fighter duties, including with 25 Squadron. During his conversion course, Joe flies in both the Blenheim Mk I – powered by two Bristol Mercury VIII engines (840hp) – and the Mk IV powered by two Bristol Mercury XV (995hp). The primary purpose of both was to familiarise him with handling two engines rather than one and, most importantly, to introduce and master the potentially lethal difficulties of asymmetric flying, with only one engine producing the thrust. He rounds off his conversion with a first solo (a couple of circuits) on a Beaufighter, on 30th November 1941. The Beaufighters had started arriving a few months previously and would eventually supplant the Blenheims for OTU training.

Totals for Nov 41 – No 2 OTU RAF Catfoss:
10 Day sorties, 13.05 hrs. Blenheim Mk I: 3.55 hrs Dual.
Blenheim Mk IV: 8.50 hrs. Beaufighter: 0.20 mins.

Having converted to twin engine flying, Joe returned to Wittering on 5 December 1941 and began to learn the art of fighting in the Beaufighter. One of the first things he would have learnt in the Mess was the sobering fact that 151 Squadron had lost six aircraft during November and December, mostly to accidents. For the first two weeks his logbook records the full gamut of practices: air interceptions on fellow squadron aircraft, using instructions from the GCI radars and from his navigator's AI, with a camera fitted to assess the results; single-engine flying; ZZ approaches[3] and 'blind' landings – staying on instruments until the last minute; 'land-aways' to get to know the local area and airfields; air-to-ground firing of the cannon; and air-to-air firing at drogues towed behind another aircraft flying out of the gunnery range at Sutton Bridge in Lincolnshire. The mission on the 18th Dec must have gone well as he records, with obvious relish:

A TO A FIRING & RETURN TO WITTERING,
SHOT DROGUE AWAY.

Joe first ventures into night flying in the Beau on 23rd December for 'Dusk landings'. As he does not fly on Christmas Eve or Christmas Day, it is possible he managed to catch some festivities. But on 27th December he teams up, for the first time, with Chris Bradshaw, 'Brad', commissioned as a Pilot Officer just a month earlier, with whom he is destined to form a successful partnership, lasting over 13 months, and a friendship lasting a lifetime. Brad was just 21 years old, born in Kew, Surrey and had joined the RAF via Cambridge University Air Squadron, having passed the first year of the Classics Tripos at Magdalene College. Brad's father was a highly respected architect who,

Inscribed by Joe on reverse: 'Hollidge, Henderson, P/O Bradshaw, Self, Cpl Winyard.
Sept 1942'. Aircrew and ground crew in front of 'their' Beaufighter aircraft.
Singleton Private Collection.

working for the Commonwealth War Graves Commission after WWI, designed some of the more iconic cemetery memorials.[4]

Now Singleton and Bradshaw are clearly considered to be an operational 25 Squadron crew as, later on 27th December, they fly their first night 'Patrol' – entered in red ink to signify they were armed and ready for interceptions. This would consist of taking their turn to provide a particular sector with fighter cover, by flying up and down under control of a GCI, who would give them vectors to fly to a target, as soon as one was spotted on the CH radars. That night, as was so very often the case, nothing happened.

Since the excitement of his scrambles in the Defiant and, albeit unsuccessful, searches for the enemy in early summer 1941, Joe had had no close contact with the enemy. He arrived on 25 Squadron in the middle of what was to prove a year or more, as far as defence of the UK was concerned, of relative quiescence. Nevertheless, he would be acutely aware that the war was not going well from a British perspective. After initial British successes in North Africa against the Italians, the Germans under Rommel were making good their losses and more. Hitler's offensives into Eastern Europe were going very much in his favour. Russia was digging in for last-ditch defence and pleading for Britain to take some pressure off them by opening a second front in the west. The only means by which this could be done was by an RAF bomber offensive, which entailed (for the same reasons of managing loss rates adopted by the Luftwaffe the previous winter) night attacks. Despite the Germans being even further behind the British in night fighter capability, they had by now built up an effective radar warning and flak defence that was inflicting serious losses on the RAF's still limited heavy bombers. The accident rate amongst the bombers was accounting for as many casualties as the German flak and fighters. Over a beer in the Mess, following another fruitless night patrol, Joe and his squadron colleagues must have viewed all this as extremely frustrating. They will surely have discussed the pros and cons of their contributing more to the offensive effort by providing fighter cover to Bomber Command. Their gloomy conclusion would or should have been that, within the current limits of their equipment, they could do little more than provide more targets for the German searchlights and flak.

Perhaps less apparent to Joe then, but later to prove so vital, was the beginnings of American involvement in the war. The US Congress had remained resolutely isolationist and neutral up to the end of 1941. In spite of this, through widespread goodwill, indirect and discrete support was being given at all levels, through a variety of channels. Wittering and 25 Squadron would see evidence of this through, for instance, new pilots arriving who had received their initial training at US Army Air Force Training Schools. American-built and -supplied aircraft were also finding their way into the RAF – the Douglas Havoc converted from Douglas DB-7 Boston bombers – arriving on the Turbinlite Flight, being one such. One wonders, then, what impact the news of the Japanese attack on Pearl Harbour on 7th December 1941 (and America's consequent declaration of war on Japan and Germany), had on the night fighter squadrons and the other personnel, fighting a quiet war alongside the A1 in Leicestershire? Indeed, it may have escaped Joe's notice for a while, as 7th December was the day he resumed flying with 25 Squadron on his return from the Catfoss OTU. Whatever the impact was, they could be certain of one thing: they would be fighting their own war, in their own way, with their own equipment for the foreseeable future; America's entry was of great strategic significance, but way above their tactical world.

And so Joe's 1942 starts routinely enough: a day sortie to check out the aircraft and equipment – mainly the AI – followed by an uneventful night patrol to protect the industrial Midlands. After 3rd January, Brad disappears from the scene until 24th February, to be replaced by a Sergeant Henderson. It was not uncommon at that time for a navigator to be sent on courses to learn and/or help develop the latest/ next version of the AI, during quiet periods on the squadron. The first centimetric AI radars were being trialled around this time,[5] destined to replace the Mk IVs in current squadron use. After flying with Sgt Henderson for a week, there is a 10-day gap until Joe records the move of 25 Squadron, from Wittering to Ballyhalbert in Northern Ireland, on 25th January. Following on a little behind, perhaps on returning from a spot of leave, Joe ferries Beaufighter 4633 from Wittering to join the rest of the Squadron.

RAF Ballyhalbert

(25th January–16th May 1942)

Ballyhalbert, situated immediately adjacent to the east coast of the Ards Peninsula, was opened in June 1941 for the purpose of protecting, primarily, the industrial facilities of Belfast, which suffered serious bomb damage in the spring of 1941. When the Beaufighters of 25 Squadron arrived to provide night fighter cover, the resident 504 Squadron Spitfires moved to the satellite airfield of RAF Kirkistown, eight miles to the south. The airfield was renowned for sudden changes in the weather, causing a high accident rate amongst the fuel-limited day fighters. Indeed, 25 Squadron lost two Beaufighters with crews on 11th February and 16th April 1942 to 'causes other than operations' – probably accidents. Joe and Sergeant Henderson's first task is to get to know the area and the GCI operators they would be working with for the next few months. They fly their first operational patrol from there on 9th February. Without explanation, on 17th and 18th February, Joe records flying a Defiant from Ballyhalbert to RAF Eglington – a Spitfire base, primarily concerned with convoy protection, on the far side of the Province, near Derry and the Irish border. On the first occasion he returns with a Pilot Officer Froggart, otherwise he flies the transits solo.

When Brad catches up with the rest of his Squadron in Ballyhalbert, he resumes flying with Joe on 26th February followed by a routine operational patrol on the 27th. March is another quiet month, with over a week with no flying and less than 10 hours flown. On the 30th, however, Joe and Brad land and spend the night at RAF Nutts Corner near Belfast which may signify a change in tack for 25 Squadron. Notorious for hastily erected half-round tin accommodation and widely dispersed facilities (a mile walk for meals), Nutts Corner is not a likely venue for a sociable land-away. It was, however the home of Coastal Command's 120 Squadron, flying B 24 Liberators, recently supplied by the USA for U-boat hunting. That the intention was to liaise with 120 Squadron, with a view to increasing Fighter Command's contribution to the Battle for the Atlantic (still going distinctly in Hitler's favour), is evidenced in the days following the visit by Joe and Brad. April 1942 is marked by a surge in activity resulting in over 52 hours flown and significant new activities. Interspersed with operational patrols, where no enemy contacts are recorded, Joe begins live firing practice with both cannon and machine gun, not only on air-to-air targets with which he was familiar, but also on air-to-sea and air-to-ground targets. This new role of air-to-surface attack is almost certainly in recognition of 25 Squadron's proximity to the U-boats and their support vessels. Although only practices are recorded, including some of which he is evidently pleased to record how many shots he got on target, these are to prove important much later in Joe's war. There is one other, albeit cryptic, hint that Joe was involved in more than repetitive night fighter training. On 8th April, he records that, during an operational patrol with GCI co-operation he had:

2 VISUALS ON HEDUP 38

It remains unclear what a 'Hedup 38' actually refers to, but the boffins developing AI at this time were beginning to experiment with head-up ('hedup' may, therefore, be a misspelling or abbreviation) displays for pilots. By placing an AI tube within the pilot's field of view, the aim was that the pilot could see the radar contacts for himself which would preclude the need for his navigator to 'talk' him into an attacking position. Unbeknown to aircrew then, this technology – the Head-Up Display (HUD) projected onto the windscreen – would become a fundamental feature of all fighters in the future. In 1942, it was a long way from fruition and was viewed with a great deal of scepticism and suspicion, not least among the navigators, whose raison d'être it seemed to threaten. As one night fighter navigator put it:

It had been forced on Fighter Command by the experts of the Fighter Interceptor Unit.[6] *While it might have been all very well for these highly skilled pilots [at FIU], it was not very practical for the average squadron pilot. It had … an extra tube placed so that the pilot could see it and could carry out the final stages of the interception himself. All the navigator needed to do was to read out the range. At night the pilot had his hands full enough without giving him an extra tube to look at. Then too, when he should have been searching the sky for a visual, he would have to look at the indicator tube. Apart from [this], the equipment suffered from very serious limitations that were not discovered until we had been struggling with it for several months.*[7]

The first half of May 1942 follows a similar pattern to April. Then on 16th May another squadron move takes place, with Joe and Brad, accompanied in their jump seat by LAC Vince (most likely squadron ground crew), flying to their new home of RAF Church Fenton in Yorkshire, where Joe had instructed on 54 OTU, in the first half of 1941.

5.

Finally into the Fight

(16th May 1942–30th September 1942)

RAF Church Fenton

(16th May 1942–16th June 1943)

Almost immediately on arriving at Church Fenton Joe is promoted to Flying Officer but, for rather different reasons, the adrenalin levels of 25 Squadron begin to rise. On their first two operational patrols, Joe and Brad make contact with the Luftwaffe. The first, on 19th May records:

> *PATROL – CHASED BANDIT, G.C.I. FAILED.*

The second, on 21st May:

> *PATROL. WORKED WITH RECLO.*
> *– MADE CONTACT BUT TOO FAST.*

The inference is that they were given vectors onto a 'bogey' (suspected enemy aircraft) by ground radar stations on both occasions. In the first instance the GCI failed, losing the contact before Brad picked it up on his AI. In the second, he got AI contact but the Beaufighter was unable to close the gap sufficiently for Joe to get the visual identification required to open fire. This was a recurrent theme when the relatively slow Beau was pitted against the more recent of the Luftwaffe bombers. Brad, who sat under a blister canopy on the spine of the Beaufighter behind Joe, was probably equipped with the AI Mk VII and would be staring intently at the small screen, being fed signals from the 'thimble' radome in the nose. In early June 1942, Joe and Brad tried another type of cooperation using both ground radar and searchlights. Denoted as '*SMACK EXERCISE/PATROL*', the concept was to fly to the start point – a searchlight pointing vertically upwards – and orbit there until the GCI radar detected an incoming bogey, directed the searchlights in that direction until the target could be 'coned' by multiple searchlights, facilitating the task of directing the Beaufighter to the target and identifying it for engagement.

At least that was the theory. The 'Smack' techniques had been used for some time by Hurricanes and Spitfires, not equipped with AI, and this was presumably an attempt to combine the best features of radar-laid searchlights and AI. It does not appear to have been very successful. No contacts are recorded during Joe's three Smack sorties and they are not repeated.

RAF Cranage – No 2 School of Air Navigation

(10th–20th June 1942)

On 10th June 1942, Joe departs Church Fenton to attend a ten-day pilot's Air Navigation Course at RAF Cranage, near Middlewich in Cheshire. The AI took up so much of a Beaufighter navigator's time and attention, that it was very difficult for him to also keep full tabs on the aircraft's position. Getting back to base after a patrol and chase was, therefore, very much a full crew activity. The more the pilot had an understanding of basic navigation, the more he could contribute to the problem. Hence pilots usually went on navigation courses during

Bristol Beaufighter – loading the cannons. Wikimedia Commons.

Mk VIIIA radar in nose of Beaufighter. Wikimedia Commons.

Beaufighter navigator position.

Beaufighter navigator's A1.

Beaufighter navigator's cockpit.

their first months on a squadron. Joe completed the course, which included two sorties in a School's Anson. The Chief Instructor of No. 2 School of Air Navigation – Wing Commander R. G. Musson – signed Joe off the course in his logbook. A little over a year later Musson, who had been an England cricketer between the wars, died when his Wellington crashed into the cliffs, in fog, near Hartland Point in Devon, whilst returning from an anti-U-boat mission, killing all eight on board.

Joe returns to squadron flying on 21st June and the following day flies with Brad to RAF Snaith, just 10 miles south east and home to 150 Squadron flying Wellingtons. Joe records flying with a Flight Lietenant Shepherd (of 150 Squadron?) for two hours at night on '**BOMBER CO-OP WITH WELLINGTON OF 150 SQD**', before returning later that night to Church Fenton. This is the first indication from Joe's record that Fighter Command is beginning to look for ways to help Bomber Command's night offensive. Since Air Marshal Sir Arthur 'Bomber' Harris was appointed Commander-in-Chief in February 1942, Bomber Command had significantly stepped up the offensive and by 21st June several '1,000 bomber raids' had already taken place, but losses amongst crews and aircraft were high. This was undoubtedly the main topic of conversation during the briefing for this sortie, with the losses very close to home for 150 Squadron, whilst Joe and Brad were only too aware of the minimal contact 25 Squadron was having with the enemy. There was, however a strict limit on what the night fighters could do to help, in terms of close escort for the bombers. It was believed (quite correctly, as it later transpired) that the AI developments the UK boffins had produced were far in advance of anything the Luftwaffe had yet devised. It was therefore absolutely vital to the war effort that no night fighter was shot down over enemy-held territory, because of the danger of losing the vital technological advantage. Regardless of how much the night fighters were itching to help the hard-pressed bombers (and they were), there was a blanket ban on them flying anywhere that might afford the remotest possibility of their precious AI ending up in German hands. Indeed, so secret was the equipment that almost no one, outside of the night fighter world, was aware of its existence let alone its purpose. Thus, many a bomber crew member, unaware of the restrictions, bitterly criticised the fighter escorts for deserting the bomber streams, precisely at the onset of great danger – on approaching the enemy coast.

Breaking from the normal squadron routine, on 23rd June, Joe flies a Magister (most likely a squadron or station 'hack'[1]) to Salmesbury in Lancashire. The reason is not recorded, but his parents living just down the road from there may have had something to do with his destination. Intriguingly, the following day, immediately after take-off to return to Church Fenton, his Magister develops engine trouble and he is obliged to spend another night there. The remainder of June is taken up with routine night flying tests (NFT) and uneventful camera-recorded patrols, coordinated by sector controllers with exotic call signs such as 'Beeswing' and 'Step-in'.

July 1942 is a busy and varied month: various cross-country sorties, usually dropping off or picking up a passenger; gunnery practice both air-to-air and air-to-ground; dual instruction in the Magister to enable fellow squadron pilots to use the hack; all intersperse the day NFT sorties to prepare for night patrols. On the 18th Joe and Brad carry out a day sortie recorded as: '*SCRAMBLE – PATROL 14,000*'. Most of the sortie is flown in cloud, so it seems it is an unsuccessful attempt to help out the day fighters with an AI platform. On the 24th they carry out a four-hour '**SEARCH FOR SGT WELSH & P/O PIZEY – NOTHING.**' This was the crew of a missing 25 Squadron aircraft, thought to have been shot down by another Beaufighter, going down in the sea near Bridlington and Joe was looking for life rafts or wreckage. A Pilot Officer Gerald Pizey is commemorated at the Runnymede memorial for airmen with unknown graves, as having died on 23rd July 1942. Finally, on 29th July, Joe and Brad make contact with the enemy – for the first time in two months – with unfortunate results:

> *PATROL. – VISUAL ON HE. 111. READY*
> *TO FIRE WHEN SEAT COLLAPSED.*

Dornier Do 217s. Photo courtesy German Federal Archives

Aircraft seats have a mechanism whereby the seat can be raised or lowered to suit the back length of the pilot. If the bolt is not fully engaged in the anchoring hole, any g-force applied to it could instantly drop the seat to the fully lowered position, the pilot's eyes going with it. This appears to be what happened. Occurring at a moment of great tension and concentration as it did, it no doubt tested Joe's bank of expletives. The Heinkel, which was faster than the Beau anyway, must have got away in the ensuing confusion. Once he had got over the shock, there would surely have been a great deal of beer-fuelled mirth in the Mess at Joe's expense. July ended with over 70 hours flown.

For the first three weeks of August it was back to the routine of fruitless patrols marked by comments such as *NO TRADE* and *STOOGED AROUND*. Then on the night of 23rd/24th August, he finally comes face-to-face with the Luftwaffe. Following a three-hour sortie Joe records:

PATROL. – DOGFIGHT WITH 217. – DAMAGED HIM
(SOMEWHERE NR BOURNE) (CAMBRIDGE).

Joe's account of the event is that he and Brad took off from Church Fenton at 2151 hrs and, under the control of Neatishead GCI, were directed to the area of Spalding in Lincolnshire. Brad obtained AI contact on a bogey flying at 10,000 ft, thought to be a Dornier 217, although positive identification was difficult due to cloud cover. Following a chase, during which the enemy took violent evasive action and returned fire, at 2235 hrs Joe eventually closed to 300 yards astern, opened fire again and saw evidence of strikes on the Dornier's port wing. At this point Joe was out of ammunition and he lost the enemy at 3,000 ft in cloud. Sometime later, a Dornier 217 crashed in East Walton Wood, Pentney, six miles east of King's Lynn, and was totally destroyed, killing all four crew members. Although several sources connect this Dornier with Joe's account, there remains a dispute as to who was actually responsible for bringing it down. Flying Officer H. G. S. Wyrill of 255 Squadron in a Beaufighter Mk VI,[2] flying in support of 12 Group from Honiley in Warwickshire and under the control of Langtoft GCI, claimed (through Langtoft) to have damaged that particular Do 217 some 50 minutes (2325 hrs) after Joe's claim. If, indeed, his account was correct (that the crash did not occur until 2325 hrs), it was unlikely the crew of the Dornier managed to stay airborne for 50 minutes after losing contact with Joe, yet remain within 50 miles), and he may have had a strong case; but there was no corroboration of the Langtoft controller's statement. In later years, Joe researched the event himself. Quoting the 9 Group's[3] Operational Record Book, he hand-writes:

> *The weather over No 12 Gp was also poor and 2 Beaufighters of No 255 Sqn were ordered to reinforce No 12 Gp and were handed to Digby. (In) One of these aircraft, F/O WYRILL effected 6 interceptions and in the ensuing combat 2 – 217s were damaged. Patrols were also flown by 256 and 96 Sqns, in addition to a further 2 Beaus from 55 Sqn. The E/A entered the Gp area at 2240 and all had left by 2310 hrs.*

By implication, Joe appears to doubt that Wyrill's account could be substantiated, because the enemy had left the area by the time of his claim. This sort of confusion over claims and accounts of events, by different crews and squadrons from different groups, operating under different sector controllers, was very common. Whatever the reality, there can be no doubt that there would be much celebrating at finally breaking their duck – an officially recorded 'Claim' – on landing back at Church Fenton, 45 minutes into 24th August.

On 28th August he is airborne again on patrol with Brad, but on this occasion he records: '*AI BLEW UP.*' With the AI sets still in development, failures could be quite spectacular smoke- and fire-generating events. Joe flew over 40 hours in August 1942, but more importantly, he was scoring at last.

In the late summer of 1942, with his advances into Russia and North Africa yet to run into trouble, Hitler sought to exact some retribution for the US day bombing offensive (now in full swing), adding to the RAF's night offensive, with some night raids of his own. The night fighter squadrons were finally getting the chance they had longed for: to make a real contribution to the war effort. Joe did not have to wait long for his own chance, which he took with both hands. On 2nd September he takes off with Brad and simply records:

1 HE 111 DESTROYED.

The combat report describes how a Flight Lieutenant Trollope of the Chain Home Low system at Easington[4] directed them to patrol off Flamborough Head, until the target was detected inbound by Easington. Thereafter, there appears to have been a textbook pick-up by Brad on the AI, closing to about 100 yards to effect identification. One short burst at the Heinkel, which was unwisely taking insufficient evasive manoeuvres, appears to have hit the bombs it was carrying. Taking care to report that one or other of them kept visual contact with the Heinkel from the opening hits to burning wreckage on the sea, with circumstantial corroboration by the Observer Corps and with no counter-claims, Joe and Brad were able to get a confirmed 'Destroyed' assessment.

Heinkel He 111 Photo courtesy German Federal Archives.

Following a short period of patrols with no trade (although an unusually high number of air tests and, intriguingly, regular air-to-surface gunnery practice), on 17th September his logbook states:

> *PATROL. – STBD ENGINE HOLED.*
> *DO. 217 DAMAGED NR KINGS LYNN.*

This was a much more confused and complex engagement than his previous one, but Flight Lieutenant Trollope[5] at Easington CHL was once again the instigator. After take-off at night, Trollope gave Joe and Brad vectors to a bandit, but the confusion started when it was realised (or believed) that Orby[6] GCI had also vectored another fighter on to the same target, so the pursuit was called off. Shortly thereafter, however, Joe spotted flares and incendiary bombs being dropped and (apparently on his own initiative) he went to investigate. Brad picked up a contact on his AI but, whilst closing, the position of the moon, the light from the flares, and inadvertent tracking by friendly searchlights on the hunter rather than the hunted, worked in

Inscribed by Joe on the reverse: 'Sept 1942 Hodgkinson, Henderson, Hollidge – My ground crew'. Singleton Private Collection.

the enemy's favour. Joe was unable to make a positive identification (vital since he was well aware there were friendly fighters around) and the bandit obviously saw Joe's Beaufighter as he opened fire and started manoeuvring violently. Having now positively identified the bandit as a Do217, in the ensuing chase and dogfight, Joe managed to get off three short bursts at close range. He saw some strikes on the enemy's fuselage, but lost contact with him around the Hunstanton/Kings Lynn area. Despite his starboard engine being holed by the Dornier's guns, it does not appear to have had any effect on the aircraft's performance.

For both of Joe's engagements and for the majority of their sorties during September 1942, he and Brad were flying Beaufighter 7824, an aircraft they had clearly established as their own. It was common practice, as far as practicable, for crews to fly the same aircraft. All aircraft and their systems have their own quirks and foibles which familiarity goes a long way to overcoming. In particular for Brad, each AI (still in the early stages of development) had significant, if subtle, differences that took some time to work around. Similarly, Joe would become comfortable with certain anomalies, for instance engine

25 Squadron Aircrew outside Officers' Mess RAF Church Fenton, September 1942.
Joe is fifth from left, excluding CO's dog. Singleton Private Collection.

instrument indications, which might preoccupy a pilot seeing them for the first time. Likewise, each aircraft and crew would be assigned, whenever possible, the same team of ground crew who got to know that particular aircraft and its idiosyncrasies, increasing the efficiency with which they kept it serviceable. Thus, Joe regarded his team as 'my ground crew'.

The photograph showing officer aircrew of 25 Squadron enjoying the late summer sunshine on the steps of Church Fenton Mess, bearing in mind that at least half of the Squadron's aircrew would be NCOs (both pilots and navigators), probably represents a large proportion of the squadron's officers. The Commanding Officer – Wing Commander 'Flash' Harry Pleasance (standing left) – had arrived on the squadron 20 months earlier in the rank of Squadron Leader as the Flight Commander, already with a DFC to his name, from his time on Blenheims during the battle for France. He was promoted into the Commanding Officer's job six months later, when his predecessor, Richard Atcherley was seriously injured in a Beaufighter crash. Pleasance had five kills on Beaufighters, for which he had been awarded a bar to the DFC. At the time of the photograph, he was in the process of handing over command of 25 Squadron to Wing Commander E. G. Watkins. Pleasance retired as a Group Captain and died in 2004 aged 90. Fourth from the right in the photo, in front of the half-hidden Brad, is Flight Lieutenant 'Inky' Inkster, a good friend of Joe's who was already aware that he has been gazetted for promotion in November 1942, to become one of 25's Flight Commanders. He would later go on to command 515 Mosquito Squadron with a unique (for the time) electronic counter-measure role to escort bombers and jam enemy ground and fighter-borne radars.

The mood of the group appears relaxed, reflecting the low tempo of operations, their recent successes and the knowledge that the Squadron was about to take delivery of an exciting new aeroplane. About the time of the photograph, on 26th September, the BBC Home Service, for the first time, revealed the existence of the 'Wooden Wonder' – the Mosquito, which had been in operational service as a high-speed light bomber (B IV) for just a few months. 105 Squadron hit the headlines with a daring set-piece attack at low level, by four Mosquitos (three returned), on the Gestapo headquarters in Oslo. The BBC was economical with the truth about the dubious military success of the raid, but did not waste the golden opportunity for some public morale boosting, by announcing the entry into the war of a bomber that could out-run German fighters. Night fighter versions of the Mosquito had begun to quietly slip into Church Fenton from late August and were in their hangars being worked on, to bring them up to operational readiness. 25 Squadron were doubtless itching to get their hands on them. Flash Pleasance was going to miss all the excitement of the new toys for the boys.

Before getting sight of the Mosquito, however, Joe flies into RAF Grantham on 6th October to spend a few days with Bomber Command. During his stay, he flies two sorties as second pilot in a Lancaster carrying out low-level cross country and fighter affiliation exercises. A logical explanation would be that he was passing on low-flying and fighter techniques to bomber pilot colleagues prior to their carrying out the Le Cruesot Raid on 17th October, when 94 Lancasters attacked at low-level the Schneider armaments factory in France. This was the first of a series of daring low-level attacks emanating from 5 Group, including the Dam Busters raid in March 1943.

So, less than a year after joining 25 Squadron, Joe is about to bid farewell to the Beaufighter, for which he had no doubt developed considerable affection and in which he had survived a few near misses. Take, for instance, Beaufighter X7706: in line with the policy of flying the same aircraft as much as possible, from 26th June to 31st July 1942, Joe and Brad flew that airframe 31 times, before taking a week's leave. Returning to flying on 10th August, they were allocated X7626. On that same day X7706 crashed. The Squadron record simply states:

10/8/42 Beaufighter X7706. Crashed, not due to enemy action. Crew killed.

During the year November 1941 to November 1942, 25 Squadron lost four aircraft and crews to accidents; a further two aircraft with their crews were posted as 'Missing on Operations'. Many more aircraft were damaged in accidents; some beyond repair and many of the crews were injured.

6.

Enter the Mossie

(1st October 1942–8th April 1943)

The Mosquito

In January 1943, Hermann Goering is alleged to have said to his staff:

> In 1940, I could at least fly as far as Glasgow in most of my aircraft, but not now! It makes me furious when I see the Mosquito. I turn green and yellow with envy. The British, who can afford aluminium better than we can, knock together a beautiful wooden aircraft that every piano factory over there is building, and they give it a speed which they have now increased yet again. What do you make of that? There is nothing the British do not have. They have the geniuses and we have the nincompoops. After the war is over I'm going to buy a British radio set – then at least I'll own something that has always worked.[1]

Like the Defiant, Blenheim and Beaufighter, the last thing their designers had in mind when developing the Mosquito was night fighting. In the frenetic build-up of the RAF during the mid-1930s, Geoffrey de Havilland envisaged a twin-engined light (up to about 1000 lb bomb load) bomber with a range of about 1500 miles, which would be fast enough to out-pace any fighter of the day. His thinking was that, if this bomber could get away from anything chasing it, then it did not need heavy defensive armour or gun turrets to slow it down aerodynamically. Furthermore, he believed that such a bomber could be made from wood that was in plentiful supply, rather than aluminium or steel for the structural strength. Thus, it would have a much greater power-to-weight ratio and it would make far fewer calls on the hard-pressed supplies of strategic materials. Whilst acknowledging these advantages, the Air Ministry were decidedly lukewarm to the concept of a light bomber, embedded as they were in the doctrine of unescorted bombers with much heavier payloads and self-defences, despite the consequent loss of speed. De Havilland nevertheless persevered and in 1940 got clearance to proceed with the development of the Mosquito, more with a view to its potential use as a high-flying photoreconnaissance platform than as a bomber. Despite development being interrupted during the Battle of Britain, in order that de Havilland factories could devote all their capacity to supporting day fighter and training aircraft production, prototypes[2] began flying in late 1940. With the need for night fighters becoming ever more apparent, it was soon recognised that the Mosquito was large enough to be fitted with an AI. In addition, its speed, range and agility would make it a much more capable replacement for the Beaufighter. So, by little more than happenstance, these two aircraft would form the mainstay of the RAF's night-fighting capability for the entire war, despite neither having been intended for that purpose.

157 Squadron at Castle Camps near Cambridge was the first squadron to receive the Mosquito modified for night fighting (designated NF II) as early as December 1941. After another abortive attempt to use them as Turbinlight aircraft, they were again modified and equipped with the AI Mk IV and 157 became operational, amid great secrecy, by the end of April 1942. Lewis Brandon[3] describes his first encounter with the Mossie (as they were widely known to their aircrew):

In the night fighter version the pilot and navigator sat side by side in a reasonably roomy cockpit, with the navigator to the right of the pilot and slightly behind him. This time the AI had been installed in such a manner that it faced forward. This was altogether a much friendlier arrangement than the Beau, as well as being more

De Havilland Mosquito NF Mk.II 157 Squadron RAF, 1942. Image courtesy Clavework Graphics.

practical for the teamwork which was such an essential part of night fighting. The Mossie was manoeuvrable, comfortable, reliable and proved to be readily adaptable for the various modifications that became necessary as more and more demands were made upon it. The cockpit layout was excellent, although perhaps a trifle cramped when both crew were above average size … Entry and exit were effected through a small door on the right hand side of the cockpit, and a collapsible steel ladder was carried inside, as the door was some eight feet from the ground when stationary. The AI equipped fighter was armed with four 20mm cannons [Hispano], which were belt fed. Their muzzles were just under the nose of the aircraft, [in which it] carried four machine guns [.303 Brownings].[4]

On 24th October 1942, Joe flies an Oxford with himself and Brad, together with another 25 Squadron crew – Pilot Officer Guyton and Flight Sergeant Hindle – to Wittering. Presumably, as it was at the heart of night fighter development (as previously mentioned), Wittering was able to use some of its Mosquitos to introduce newcomers to the type. From there, the following day, Joe's first flight in a Mossie is as a passenger with a Flight Lieutenant Bodien,[5] indicating that this was not a two-stick T3 training version (which probably had not yet arrived on the front line), but a regular NF II. The fifteen minutes sitting alongside Bodien in the navigator's seat was apparently sufficient to enable Joe to go off later that day, and the following day, to get to know the aircraft and its weapon systems. Returning to Church Fenton on 27th October, the next two weeks are taken up with checking out fellow pilots on the 25 Squadron Mosquitos, first by day then by night, and also getting in some Mosquito AI and gunnery practice with Brad. Interspersing these, Joe and Brad continue to fly fruitless operational night patrols in Beaufighter 7824; their last being on 8th November 1942. From then on, the Mossie replaces the Beau as the aircraft of choice for night fighting operations, as far as Joe is concerned. It does not, however, change the tempo of their war, which shows the same frustrating pattern: a dearth of customers and vectors on to bogeys that turn out to be friendly. Flying around 30–40 hrs each month and evidently being able to take a few days off now and again may have seemed a relatively pleasant existence. But the impatience of 25 Squadron to try out their shiny new fleet of Mosquitos against the Luftwaffe would have been growing by the day.

The news from North Africa – where the RAF had now established air superiority enabling Montgomery to embark on pushing Rommel's Axis armies ever westwards, and whispers of Mosquito bombers' early successes – would only have fuelled the impatience. In the same way Joe and Brad had made 7824 their very own Beau (Joe's last flight in her is to Salmesbury and back on 30th November), from the beginning, they were allotted to Mosquito 752 to iron out the wrinkles. Nevertheless, it would seem that the Squadron had at least one T3 dual-control aircraft available by the end of November – on the 28th Joe flies a 1.40 dual sortie with a Pilot Officer Hogarth. From then on it is increasingly clear that Joe, with his Flying Instructor background, is periodically checking out the new arrivals on the piloting mysteries of the Mosquito. Joe's second Christmas on 25 Squadron appears to have been an even more relaxed period than his first, with a whole six days off flying starting on Christmas Eve and returning on the 30th December to fly a night patrol with Brad. On New Year's Eve he flies one short day sortie for pilot training and has New Year's Day off. As they saw the New Year in, the whole of 25 Squadron must have been chomping at the bit for a more productive 1943. They did not have to wait long. The first two weeks were pilot instruction, air-to-air gunnery practice and patrols during which, on 12th January, Joe is promoted to Acting Flight Lieutenant. Then on 15th January 1943, at last they are able to test their Mossie against the enemy:

PATROL. – DO. 217. DAMAGED –
3 SQUIRTS – HIT ON 1ST AND 3RD.

On a clear brightly moonlit night, Joe and Brad take off in 752 and, receiving vectors from Easington CHL, pick up a violently weaving contact on the 'PI' (Pilot Indicator) of the Mk V AI. Closing to 50 yards, both Joe and Brad identify it as a Dornier 217, whereupon Joe gives a short burst and Brad reports seeing hits on the tail unit of the enemy, which promptly dives steeply to port with Joe following. Another opportunity presents itself for a pot shot from 150 yards but no hits are seen. On closing from astern the Dornier for a third time, both Joe and Brad must have received a tremendous shock when, unannounced, 752 suddenly flips on her back and starts vibrating severely. Fighting to bring his aircraft back on an even keel, Joe notices a red light has illuminated on his port undercarriage indicator in the cockpit. From this he concludes that his port undercarriage leg has become unlocked from the fully up position but, despite the continuing bone-shaking vibration, he presses on with a third attack. Another short burst from 50 yards astern and to port results in further strikes seen between the Dornier's port engine and fuselage. The vibration now causes his radio to start failing and, although he is desperate to pursue the Dornier to confirm the kill and go looking for more, the unknown damage to his own aircraft forces him to turn for home.

An examination after landing back at Church Fenton revealed that the starboard undercarriage nacelle door was damaged, causing the control difficulties and vibration. As no return fire at all had been seen from the Dornier, the conclusion was that the initial high-speed chase had caused the undercarriage door to fly open, with the alarming result. Despite only being able to claim 'Damaged' this was 25 Squadron's first claim in the Mosquito NF II. No doubt there followed great celebrations in Church Fenton's messes and local inns, but whether that explains the six-day gap before Joe and Brad fly again is anybody's guess.

That this attack was carried out using the AI Mk V, complete with Pilot Indicator is interesting. Lewis Brandon, a Mosquito navigator, is less than impressed with this latest development of the AI:

> *Fighter Command had perpetrated a blunder almost as bad as the Turbinlite fiasco. They had decided to install in our beautiful Mossies, in fact in all the first batch of Mossies to reach the squadrons, a wretched new Mark of AI. This was the Mark 5 AI which had all the faults of the Mark 4 [which Joe and Brad were very familiar with from the Beau], plus many of its own ... it was rather like going back to the divining rod. There were times ... when I thought that if I took a hazel twig, persuaded a Dachshund to lift a leg against it and then took the twig into the Mossie with me, it would lead me to a German more readily than would a Mark 5 AI...*

As mentioned in relation to the 'HED-UP 38' display in the Beaufighter, Brandon's distaste for the Mark V may have had as much to do with his perceived threat of side-lining the navigator, as with the actual effectiveness of the kit. In any event, on this occasion the Mark V appears to have performed well up to expectations, but what Brad thought of this pilot-oriented AI is not known.

Subsequent research by Chris Goss ties in Joe's claim with a Dornier 217 E of Kampfegeschwader (Battle Wing) No. 2, which went missing with a crew of four on the night of 15th January 1943. Following this success, Joe has some more down time (weather may have been a factor). Returning on the 21st, he flies a NFT day sortie with Brad, in the unfamiliar airframe HJ 918. The remainder of January passes uneventfully, with a relatively low count of 21 hours flown.

February begins rather differently. Brad is not in evidence for the first two weeks, so Joe flies with a variety of navigators, but 752 is still the airframe of preference. The two patrols he carries out before Brad gets back, however, are both with a Flying Officer Osborne. The first on 4th February he describes a familiar frustration:

PATROL – TRADE BOGEY TURNED FRIENDLY.

The second, on 6th February, is different but no more satisfying:

SEARCHLIGHT CO-OP – VERY BORING CLOVER LEAF.

On the same day, he has entered:

S/L 'BILL' CARNABY & HECTOR KEMP,
TAIL CAME OFF & WENT STRAIGHT IN.

Like Brad, but a few years prior, Bill Carnaby had learnt to fly with Cambridge University Air squadron, where he studied Economics and Law at Christ's College. He joined the RAF in 1935 and had survived the decimation of his Defiant Squadrons (264 and 85) during the Battle of France and the early part of the Battle of Britain, before Defiants were withdrawn. He was now a Flight Commander on 25 Sqn and clearly suffered a catastrophic structural failure of his Mosquito, 2 miles east of Church Fenton, shortly after take-off. No doubt the Squadron, in particular the officers who were all very close and not least Joe and Brad, would have been devastated at his ill-fortune, after all he had come through. It certainly would not have escaped Joe and Brad's notice that they had flown the aircraft that failed – HJ 918 – just two weeks before. Such failures were mercifully very rare, but were also completely unpredictable as to which manoeuvre would break the camel's back; so it was another there-but-for the-grace-of-God moment for Joe.

The remainder of February was busy (over 33 hours flown) and varied with air tests, aerobatics, air-to-surface firing practice, land-aways to Ouston and Driffield and, unusually a day scramble, for which he records:

SCRAMBLE TO 29,000' KEPT
OUT OF WAY BECAUSE OF SPITS.

Since the day fighters would normally not require back-up from the night fighters, it is unclear why Joe was involved. Perhaps the Spitfires had a problem that the Sector Controller thought merited calling on the Mosquitos, but the problem was resolved before Joe could engage. Another intriguing diversion comes on the 15th when Joe flies with an LAC Joyce in a Miles Martinet, which is a ruggedized version of the Master and Joe clearly did not need to be checked out – he just got in and flew it. Where the Martinet came from and why he should suddenly turn his hand to target towing are mysteries but, if for amusement, it was not too successful. Even though he records flying for 25 minutes, he also notes:

DROGUE TOWING – EXERCISE CANCELLED.

In the latter half of February, the emphasis for Joe and Brad appears to be shifting away from those endless hours of unproductive night patrols to low-level cross-country navigational practice both by day and by night. The reason becomes apparent on the 20th when he records:

TO COLTISHALL FOR 'RANGER' OPS.
(WEATHER U/S FOR 4 DAYS.)

It also explains why, on both Beaufighters and Mosquitos, the crews were expected to keep their hands in with periodic air-to-surface firing practice: the Powers That Be had always intended that such capable aircraft should not be constricted solely to defensive operations. We have seen that Goering's mind-set at this time was making significant Luftwaffe forays as far north as Yorkshire a rarity indeed; the Mosquito night fighters had become victims of their own publicity and success. It was time for 25 Squadron to go on the offensive. That said, on returning from Coltishall, the new modus operandi, for Joe at least, has to go on to the back-burner for a couple of months. It was time for Brad to move on and for Joe again to work up his crew to operational status with a new navigator. On 1st March 1943, flying in trusty 752, Joe records:

Exit Fg Off 'Brad' Bradshaw...   *...Enter Plt Off Geoff Haslam – March 1943. Singleton Private Collection.*

PATROL. – NO TRADE – VERY HECTIC GCI
WITH G HOGARTH[?]. (BRAD'S LAST PATROL.)

The following day, they flew their last sortie together – a land-away to RAF Ford, home of the Fighter Intercept Unit. Were they delivering Brad's kit to his next posting? Brad flew with Joe on over 200 Beaufighter sorties and nearly 70 Mosquito sorties. Despite many long hours of patrolling Hun-less skies, together they notched up three Dornier 217s damaged, including the first 25 Sqn Mosquito claim, and one Heinkel 111 destroyed. They also forged a friendship that would last both their lifetimes.

Without further ado, Joe was teamed up with his new navigator – Pilot Officer William Geoffrey Haslam – flying their first sortie together on 4th March 1943, and their first patrol the following night. During what was to prove an exceptionally busy month (almost 56 hours flown), Joe takes his new navigator through the full gamut of Mosquito operations, day and night, offensive and defensive, air-to-air and air-to-ground. Geoff appears to make a promising early impact on Joe who is moved to remark on the 11th March:

NIGHT X-COUNTRY – VERY GOOD.

But the full gamut also included the usual complaints and gremlins. On the same night (11th):

SCRAMBLE – MANNED FORWARD
BEACON ORBIT – VERY STOOGING.

And the following night (12th):

PATROL – SCRAMBLE – UNDER MAYFLY [GCI] *– CONTACT ON*
BOGEY (FRIENDLY) – A WHITLEY [BOMBER]. *SET U/S.*

And on 15th March:

SCRAMBLE – SAW 2 HUNS SHOT DOWN.
MANNED SEARCHLIGHT BOX.

So at least there was evidence of Luftwaffe presence to keep adrenalin levels high, reinforced when, on a day GCI practice with Easington GCI, Joe records that:

HUNS APPEARED – PATROLLED ABOUT
70–80 MILES OUT [FROM COAST].

That same night more frustration:

PATROL – OPS – BLITZ ON MIDDLESBOROUGH
– NO CHASES – WEAPON BENT.

They flew a further fruitless patrol on the night of 28th March. Joe was also interspersing all these operational sorties with a variety of others, not involving Geoff. He flies Mosquito air tests, numerous land-aways including Salmesbury (another parental visit?) and dropping off an Air Vice Marshal Edmonds at Catterick, a few instructional sorties and a BABS Test with Flying Officer Osborne. He also, without explanation, on 21st March flies solo in a Hurricane for half an hour and is obviously impressed, recording:

PETE SEWELL, JOCK CAIRNS
GEORGE HOGARTH COOKIE
FREDDIE MANG, DAVE

**LOCAL [AREA] – 1 ROLL –
VERY NICE. 1–½ ROLL.**

'JOHNA', REGGIE &
JOE SINGLETON APRIL 1943.

Comrades in arms. Singleton Private Collection.

April 1943 was much less frenetic, with just over 37 hours and 7 patrols flown, but no trade offered by the Luftwaffe. Dual instruction for pilots (three sorties) and offensive training continues, including cross-country low-flying on the 18th (**'VERY GOOD'**) and on the 20th a day sortie:

**A-S [GUNNERY] & TO LECONFIELD – BOMBER
AFFILIATION – DAMNED HARD WORK (VERY HOT).**

Geoff is noticeable by his absence for the last week in April, for reasons unknown, and his place next to Joe is taken by a Sgt Skinner, clearly an experienced operator, who flies the last two of Joe's April patrols. Geoff returns to fly with Joe on a patrol on 3rd May and, on the 8th, two very different sorties. The first, 2.20 hrs by day, is annotated:

A-S FIRING. DEH'V BEAT UP AT BOLTON
– BIG FLAP! – GOOD BEAT UP.

De Havilland's Lostock factory in Bolton made, primarily, propellers and it would seem Joe had been asked to show, with a 'beat up', its workforce the front line's appreciation of their efforts. From where Joe sat, it was well received! The second, .50 hrs by night, was at the other end of the spectrum:

PATROL – CU-NIMBUS UP TO 22,000' – RETURNED – NBG.

There is no more uncomfortable flying than in highly turbulent cumulo-nimbus thunderstorm clouds, especially by night when lightning flashes and strikes heighten the chaos and threaten instant natural destruction.

From 9th April, there is a distinct change of emphasis and tempo to offensive operations, presaged but never realised before Brad departed for pastures new.

7.

From Defence to Attack

(9th April–4th June 1943)

Intruder and Ranger Operations

Intruder operations were low-level penetrations of enemy airspace, targeting specific Luftwaffe bases. They were timed to coincide with known periods of enemy scrambles or multiple recoveries, with the aim of causing as much disruption to them as possible, by attacking either the aircraft themselves or the airfield infrastructure. In more recent air warfare parlance, Intruders are recognised as Offensive Counter-Air Operations. Ranger operations were also low-level penetrations, but with no specific target other than known areas of enemy transport movements, with the aim of causing as much disruption as possible to anything moving by land, water or air. Today these would be known as Interdiction Operations. Both Intruders and Rangers were originally conceived to support bomber operations, by reducing Hitler's ability to interfere with them, and so their timing and direction was co-ordinated with bomber offensives. Later they would be used for wider purposes.

As already mentioned, the Mosquito was an ideal platform for these types of operations, having the range, speed and armaments to operate alone and at distance. Dedicated Intruder squadrons were being formed in early 1943, using bomber versions of the aircraft. It was soon recognised, however, that the spare capacity of the Mosquito NFIIs, occasioned by only sporadic defensive needs, could not be overlooked. The major snag with using night-fighter aircraft for this purpose was the AI. It was considered that the RAF's advantage in AI technology was so sensitive and critical, that running the risk of even one falling into German hands was totally unacceptable. Thus an NFII aircraft had to have its AI removed, before it could be made available for Intruder or Ranger Operations.

Another contentious issue was whether these operations should be mounted by day or by night. As most of the RAF's bombing raids were conducted at night, there were strong arguments that the associated Intruder/Ranger operations should also be by night. On the other hand, night low flying was inherently hazardous and the accident rate would inevitably be greater than by day. In addition, the identification and engagement of moving targets at night was much more difficult than by daylight. Conversely, whereas night operations were effective in a variety of weather conditions, including cloudless skies, day operations needed a quite narrow set of conditions – ideally sufficient cloud cover to reduce chances of detection and provide hiding places, yet good enough visibility below cloud to identify and attack targets. Furthermore, the US Army Air Force was operating by day and needed as much support as the RAF by night.

So it was that on 9th May 1943, despite having been on the Cu-Nim patrol the night before and, apparently, still in Yorkshire with a long transit to the south, Joe and Geoff were scrambled at 0830 hrs, in an unfamiliar airframe – Mosquito 688 minus AI. Their mission was a day Ranger over enemy-occupied territory but, doubtless in accordance with pre-ordained instructions, returned empty-handed with the rueful remark:

...CLOUD COVER RAN OUT AT DUTCH COAST.

At this point, for Geoff at least, fate intervenes to groom him for higher things and spoil the fun. As the Church Fenton Operations Record Book (ORB) says:

> *Flying Officer [Geoff had been promoted in early May] W. G. Haslam (Navigator Radio 130325) is detached to FIU Ford for a Navigator Radio Leaders course.*

On the 13th, Joe, accompanied by a Pilot Officer Burrow, set off for a location much better suited to sorties over the Channel – RAF Castle Camps on the Cambridgeshire/Essex border and home to newly specialist Mosquito Intruder Squadron – 605. That same night Joe and Burrow take off for a long (0330 hr) sortie, recorded as follows:

> *INTRUDER OPS – PATROLLED TWENTE & THEN SHORT RANGER. – ONE E/A DAMAGED AT TWENTE (AT END OF LANDING RUN). – C. CAMPS – 10 MILES N OF ALKMAR – KAMPEN – LOCHEN – TWENTE – RHEINE – TWENTE – D COAST 4 MILES NORTH OF EGMOND BASE.*

The ORB gives greater detail:

> *Flight Lieutenant J. SINGLETON took off at 0112 hours to patrol TWENTE.[1] He crossed the Dutch coast near ALKMAAR at 01.56 at 4500 feet and then proceeded to TWENTE via KAMPEN and LOCHEN arriving over the patrol area at 2000 feet at 0224 hours. Ten minutes over the aerodrome produced no signs of activity although two dummy aerodromes[2] were observed to the south. A large fire was seen to start near one of these and the MOSQUITO was brought down to 400 feet to investigate, but as no activity was seen here, course was set for RHEINE[3] at 0250 hours, but once again nothing was to be seen, and the aircraft returned to TWENTE. This time a flare path and visual LORENZ[4] were visible and an unidentified aircraft was seen approaching to land without navigation lights, but with a landing light burning. As the visual LORNZ then commenced to douse, the MOSQUITO was put into a shallow dive to make a quarter head-on attack on the aircraft, which was now almost stationary.[5] A four-second burst was given from 1000 down to 300 feet at 0315 hours and cannon*

strikes were seen to rake the machine. All the aerodrome lights were immediately doused and Flight Lieutenant SINGLETON turned for base, crossing the DUTCH coast at EGMOND at 4500 feet at 0336 hours. Tracer and flares from a naval engagement 40 miles west of THE HAGUE were seen and the MOSQUITO landed at CASTLE CAMPS at 0440 hours. One unidentified enemy aircraft is claimed as damaged and this is the first aircraft to be engaged by the Squadron on Intruder Operations.

It is interesting that the transit and patrol heights of around 4000 feet would normally be heights at which there would be a high risk from German flak, which could detect aircraft at that height, either by radar or visually. That this did not seem to be a cause for concern for Mosquitos demonstrates the value of two of its fundamental characteristics. Firstly, due to the mainly wood construction, it was relative invulnerable to German radar (such as it was). The aircraft was 'stealthy', as it would be termed 50-odd years later. Secondly, navigating at night was made infinitely easier with sufficient height for the navigator to recognise landmarks; crews could take advantage of this, because the Mosquito's basic high speed made visual engagements practically impossible for flak crews, especially at night.

Sergeant Skinner now re-joins Joe as Geoff's stand-in and they are soon into the fray again. On 15th May, they deploy to RAF Coltishall in East Anglia, this time for Ranger Operations and on the same night embark on another long sortie into enemy territory, known as Ranger Route 8. Taking detail from the Combined Intelligence and Personal Combat Report, they take off just before 2300 hrs, cross the Dutch coast just south of the island of Vlieland and head east, crossing into Germany near Oldenberg, and head for Syke.[6] A northbound train is spotted near Heiligenrode which, despite slight, inaccurate flak, they attack with 2–3 seconds of both cannon and machine gun fire. Strikes on the leading engine are observed. Proceeding to Syke, another train is attacked twice, two miles from the town, firstly with both cannon and machine guns, secondly with cannon only. Concentrated strikes are seen on the engine, which emits vivid flashes and clouds of steam before stopping. About 8 miles to the south west of Syke, near Bassum, a third northbound train is attacked three times from abeam, the first with cannon only and then with machine guns, until both are exhausted. Strikes on, and flashes emanating from, the locomotive and leading coach are observed. All these attacks are from abeam the trains, firing in a dive between 1,200 to 100 ft. Altogether, 700 rounds of armour-piercing/high-explosive cannon rounds and over 700 machine-gun rounds are expended. Escaping through Holland south of Amsterdam, Joe and Skinner land back safely, not at Coltishall but at Church Fenton around 0230 hrs on 16th May. Joe's logbook description is rather more prosaic:

3 TRAINS PRANGED SOUTH OF BREMEN.

Joe is made a War Substantive Flight Lieutenant on 17th May, that night a similar routine is followed: depart in the afternoon with Sgt Skinner for Coltishall, take off at 2300 hrs for Ranger Route 8, heading for Syke. Some 30 miles inside Germany, they report (rather coyly?) that they attack two white smoke trails with cannon and machine gun, believing them to be locomotives. It is probably in the latter stage of the attack, when at close quarters and they see their shells hit home, that they realise that the smoke is coming from very stationary factory chimneys alongside the railway line. Undaunted, they resume the search for targets on the railway line running out of Sulingen (30 miles south of Bremen). In the absence of trains, they decide to strafe the town centre with a 4–5-second burst. Some 20 miles further south, they finally sight a train heading west towards Lubbecke, which they attack and, almost immediately, a second is spotted and hit, then a third. Just to be sure, they then hit each of the three (now stationary) trains for a second time in reverse order. In all, 774 cannon and 586 machine-gun rounds are fired. The escape route and flight back are uneventful, landing at Church Fenton at 0235 hrs. Joe's version is, as usual, sardonic:

3 TRAINS PRANGED N.E. OF OSNABRUCK. 3.35.

Bombing of the Gestapo headquarters in Shellhuset house, Copenhagen by the RAF. This was Operation Carthage. This photo illustrates the incredible manoeuvrability of the Mosquito on these low-level raids involving attacks on key targets such as buildings and locomotives. Nationalmuseet (National Museum) of Denmark.

The intention was to repeat the process the following day (18th May) but, having got as far as Coltishall, the Ranger operation is cancelled due to poor weather; Joe and Skinner return to Church Fenton empty handed. However, on 23rd May they are back at Castle Camps for another Intruder operation against Twente airfield in the Netherlands.

INTRUDER OPS – PATROLLED TWENTE AERODROME – THEN RANGER UP DORTMUND-EMS CANAL – 1 TRAIN. 3.25.

Unlike the three previous occasions, the visibility over enemy territory is less than ideal, being described as 'moderate to poor' in the Combat Report. Undoubtedly this has an impact on the outcome. Before then, however, having taken off just before midnight, they encounter a common problem for these lone night raiders (although a first for Joe) – being engaged by one's own side – later to be known as 'Friendly Fire' or 'Blue-on-Blue'. Over the North Sea, some 25 miles east of the English coast, Joe reports seeing a 'bright yellow flash which seems to burst at a height of approximately 5,000 ft [they were at 4,000 ft]. This is quickly followed by the correct colours of the day (two greens) being fired from the air.'

It is not hard to envisage the heart-stopping frenzy behind these words. The crew would have been briefed before flight that the home defences had been informed of their planned activity and would let them pass unmolested. Just in case, however, they would also have been briefed on the 'colours of the day' – the agreed number and colours of signal flares, changed daily for security, fired by the aircraft navigator using a Verey pistol, to demonstrate to those on the ground that an unidentified aircraft was friendly. Whilst fine in theory, it was well known that the home anti-aircraft batteries were ultra-competitive and keen to do their bit for the war; and some messages always fail to get through. Their favourite unofficial mantras were 'Fire first, ask questions later,' and 'If it flies it dies'. The number of blue-on-blue casualties this caused in WWII is unknown but numerous; aircrews were well aware of the risks and abhorred the thought of dying at the hands of over-enthusiastic compatriots, rather than the Nazis. On this occasion, the first shot was not the lucky one, but it still takes precious time to fire and reload a Verey pistol: Sergeant Skinner would be scrambling frantically, whilst Joe, no doubt, was throwing the aircraft into violent evasive manoeuvres. And all that was before crossing the enemy coast.

Leaving that scare behind, Joe and Skinner cross the Dutch coast at 4,000 ft at half past midnight and begin a wide orbit of Twente at 2,000 ft just before 0100 hrs. For ten minutes or so, no activity is seen, apart from lights and green Vereys at the dummy airfield and the Visual Lorenz appearing briefly at Twente. It is quite likely that these are deliberate attempts by the Germans to confuse the threatening, suspicious aircraft they could hear. A large explosion is seen about 15 miles away when an unidentified aircraft crashes; searchlights, heavy flak and explosions are in evidence to the south, perhaps indicating the association of their Intruder mission with a bomber offensive, in progress overhead. Deciding that, this time, the Luftwaffe are alerted to their presence and are not going to cooperate, after half an hour over Twente, Joe decides to revert to Plan B and convert the mission to a Ranger. He crosses over into Germany in search of different prey. Heading north for about 30 miles, he sights a train moving northwards, five miles south of the town of Aschendorf. He attacks at 0144 hrs from abeam, with a 2–3-second burst with cannon and machine gun, opening at 700 ft and closing to 300 ft. Orbiting to carry out a second attack, Joe fails to locate the train again – due to the poor visibility that night. Acting on pre-flight intelligence, he heads for the town of Heppel for other targets but, again thwarted by the visibility, fails to find it, and decides to head for home. On the way, he reports seeing a lot of activity, including another unidentified aircraft crash and explode 10 miles off the Dutch coast. He lands safely at Castle Camps at 0310 hrs, having expended only 61 cannon and 70 machine-gun rounds, but claiming one locomotive damaged. After some rest, the following day they return to Church Fenton.

Joe was probably unaware at the time, but that was to be the last of his Ranger/Intruder operations. Once again his logbook entries belie the dangers and difficulties of these operations. When Flying Officer E. G. White joined 410 Squadron RCAF[7] (Mosquitos, RAF Coleby Grange south of Lincoln) in April 1943, he asked about these Ranger Ops the squadron had just started flying and was told: You fly into France, do a slow turn to port, shoot up a couple of trains, get lost and come home.

In their more blasé moments, that could be Joe or Sgt Skinner speaking, such was the charmed life they had led so far. But, like everyone involved, they were only too aware of the reality. Flying Officer White shared exactly the same good fortune on his one and only attempt to conduct a Ranger by day – the requisite cloud cover ran out at the Dutch coast and they turned back. On his second night Ranger out of West Malling in Kent (17th May – the same night Joe bagged three trains near Osnabruck), however, they were penetrating occupied France, when they unwittingly flew over a heavily defended operations centre. They were caught by searchlights, flak opened up and, despite violent evasive manoeuvres, they were hit. The aircraft was still controllable, but the compass was damaged and misreading which made for fraught navigation back across the Channel; they also had a fuel leak. They finally made it back to West Malling very short of fuel and it was only on touchdown that they discovered they also had suffered damage to the undercarriage. They '…finished up in an

The de Havilland Mosquito FB.VI NS898 'SY-Z' of 613 City of Manchester Squadron at RAF Lasham. Photo courtesy of Ringwayobserver. Wikimedia Commons.

aircraft consisting only of a cockpit, the tail having been left behind on the runway with most of the wings.'[8] Both were very fortunate to escape with only minor injuries. As a rider to the two squadrons' links, 25 Squadron loaned 410 Squadron Mosquito HJ 878, a dual-control aircraft in which Joe had flown two instructional sorties with fellow pilots on 21st April 1943. It was written off when it crashed on landing at Coleby Grange on 1st June.

Joe and Sergeant Skinner's brush with friendly flak was just one illustration that these operations were nowhere near as straightforward as they, by great skill as well as good fortune, had made them look. 25 Squadron lost at least 13 aircraft whilst on Intruder missions, not only to enemy action, but also falling victim to the inherent perils of night flying at low level – mid-air collisions, disorientation, pylons, etc. Many crews lost their lives: Flight Lieutenant Ron Cooke (seen sitting on the left of Joe in 16th June 1943 25 Squadron photograph), and his navigator Flight Sergeant Frederick Ellacott (fifth from left back row) took off from Church Fenton in DD 748[9] on the night of 30th July for an Intruder Operation to Westerland, near the Germany/

Short Sunderland flying boat. Photo courtesy Canadian Armed Forces.

Denmark border. Shortly after take-off, Ron Cooke radioed that he was returning to base with engine trouble, nothing more was heard from them. Their aircraft appears to have crashed 15 miles east of Hornsea. Ron's body was never found – so he is commemorated on the Runnymede Memorial. Flight Sergeant Ellacott's body was washed up three weeks later, with bleak irony, in Denmark. He is buried at the beautiful cemetery of Kirkeby in Jutland, alongside 27 other Commonwealth airmen.

Despite the dangers, Intruder and Ranger operations were proving to be so successful, both in support of the Combined Bomber Offensive and by disruption of the Luftwaffe's own bombing raids, that more and more dedicated squadrons were being formed. Hitler was infuriated that Goering, despite his boasts to the contrary, was powerless to stop these aircraft roaming over their territory, apparently at will and relatively unscathed. The actual damage they caused, although substantial, was rather less significant than the psychological effect on pilots and train drivers et al., who had become strangely reluctant to venture out at night, and so twitchy when they did, their own accident rate soared. Although 25 Squadron had used Mosquito IIs, modified by removing the AI for these operations and designated Mosquito IIF, in August 1943 they received a batch of eight Mosquito FB 6s.[10] As they were on squadron strength for only a month, it would seem that it was decided 25 Sqn would not become a dedicated Intruder Squadron.

Following a spot of leave, Joe resumes flying with Geoff Haslam on 2nd June 1943 (now back from his course). An extract from the 25 Squadron ORB for 4th June reads:

> Orders were received this morning that three crews, with aircraft, were to be detached for special duties at Predannack – a mysterious assignment which captured our imagination. The crews selected … spent the day preparing to go but rain and low cloud prevented their departure; indeed, the only flying which was possible [at Church Fenton] was testing of aircraft for night readiness. The day was notable for other activities … An evening cricket match between the Squadron and an Operations team was abandoned after only a few minutes' play, owing to rain. It may be said that increasing keenness is being shown by the Squadron aircrew in summer sports, cricket and tennis in particular…
>
> 5 June 1943.
> Much of the earlier part of the day was spent by the Predannack crews in briefing, swinging the compasses and re-harmonising the guns of the selected Ranger aircraft:- DZ 685, DZ 688 and DD757. By teatime the clouds had lifted and winds had freshened sufficiently for departure.

So, on the 5th, Joe and Geoff fly down to RAF Predannack, near the tip of the Lizard Peninsula in Cornwall – the southern-most airfield on the British mainland. This signalled not only a complete change of scenery, but also yet another very different type of operation – Instep Patrols.

8.

A Cornish Interlude

(5th–15th June 1943)

Instep Patrols – RAF Predannack

(2nd June 1943)

2 June 1943
A Short Sunderland of No.464 Squadron, Royal Australian Air Force is attacked over the Bay of Biscay by eight Junkers Ju 88s. The ensuing combat lasts for 45 minutes and sees the Sunderland shoot down three of the attacking Ju 88s. The Sunderland is badly damaged, with one of its crew killed and three wounded. Nevertheless, the pilot, Flight Lieutenant C. B. Walker brings the aircraft safely back and is subsequently awarded the Distinguished Service Order.

The combat indicated the seriousness with which the Germans viewed the Allied air threat to their U-boats transiting the Bay of Biscay from their French coastal ports. The Germans deployed long range Junkers Ju88s of Kampfgeschwader 40 and shorter ranged Focke Wulf Fw190 fighters to try to combat the threat of Allied aircraft. In response the Royal Air Force (RAF) deployed Bristol Beaufighter and later de Havilland Mosquito squadrons to try to counter the threat of German interceptors. The patrols became known as Instep operations. The RAF lost 15 aircraft in patrols over the Bay of Biscay during June 1943. 4 Junkers Ju88s were claimed as destroyed by Instep patrols.[1]

Joe and Geoff's detachment to 264 (Madras Presidency)[2] Sqn – the resident Mosquito squadron based at RAF Predannack in support of Coastal Command's anti-U-boat operations[3] – was short but dramatic. Joe's was the senior of three 25 Squadron crews and aircraft sent to Predannack to conduct Instep Patrols. At least three other Mosquito NFII squadrons also each sent three crews to augment the effort – 157 Squadron from RAF Bradwell Bay in Essex, 410 (Cougar) Squadron from RAF Coleby Grange and 456 Squadron from RAF Middle Wallop. As Lewis Brandon, navigator in one of the 157 Squadron crews, who arrived at Predannack at about the same time as Joe and Geoff H, puts it:

> *The anti-U-boat warfare was mounting to a crescendo at this time. Packs of U-boats were hunting out in the Atlantic, often guided by long-range aircraft[4] operating from western France. To combat the U-boat packs, Coastal Command had Sunderlands, Halifaxes and Liberators operating from Cornwall, flying out over the Atlantic to spot them. They had been having a fair amount of success, so much so that the Jerries had popped a squadron or two of Junkers 88s on the Brest Peninsula to chase Coastal Command's big boys. They, in turn, had asked Fighter Command to lend them some Mozzies to harry the Junkers 88. That was us. The next move was for some Focke Wolf 190s to arrive at Brest ... so we had our own little war in the southwest...*
>
> *When we arrived at Predannack, almost the whole of Cornwall was covered in sea mist for nearly a week [restricting flying]. With the aid of some Coastal [Command] chaps it gave us an opportunity of finding out something of our new role and working out some tactics.*
>
> *Our job was to act as long-range day fighters for patrols in the Bay of Biscay and we were to be put to any use Coastal Command needed us for ... We had been advised to fly at about a hundred feet for two reasons: we would be difficult for a vessel to see, and any other aircraft about were likely to be higher ... and would therefore be fairly easy for us to spot.[5]*

So, on the afternoon of 7th June two days after arriving, Joe and Geoff H take off from Predannack on an Instep Patrol. They are leading a four-ship formation consisting of: Flight Officer J. Cheney (pilot) with Pilot Officer J. K. Mycock (navigator) of 25 Squadron, accompanied by Flight Officer J. Newell (pilot) with Flight Sergeant A. J. Keating (navigator) and Flight Sergeant J. W. Richardson (pilot) with Sergeant T. Landy (navigator), these four being Australians from 456 Squadron.

After a long, fruitless search for enemy aircraft, at around 1830, Flight Officer Cheney sights the smoke from a two-masted steam trawler travelling at about four knots. The trawler, flying the French Tricolour, has the name Tadorne painted on the hull, is battened down with no sign of life aboard; nor are there any signs of fishing gear. Joe orders the formation to attack and records:

ATTACKED TRAWLER 'TADORNE' AT [LAT & LONG] WITH CANNON & MG (320 CANNON, 1000 MG). 4 ATTACKS LEFT IT SEVERELY DAMAGED AND SINKING.

Joe would not have taken lightly the decision to attack. Lewis Brandon describes their reaction to the same dilemma, faced by them a couple of days later:

> We had been told that the Germans were using trawlers to pass on information to their long-range aircraft or to the U-boats. There was an agreed limit of, I believe, ten or fifteen miles [from the coast] for trawlers fishing legitimately, but this chap was way outside those limits.
>
> It was a very difficult decision for the leader of our formation to make. We had been told that anything of this sort was fair game but the trawler did look defenceless. However, orders is orders, and the leader ordered an attack.

As Lewis Brandon alludes to, the weather is unusually poor for the time of year, with persistent low cloud and fog so it is not until four days later, on Friday 11th June, that the weather breaks and Joe gets airborne on his second and final Instep Patrol. This time Joe is leading a formation of six aircraft, divided into Blue (three 25 Squadron aircraft) and Green Sections (three 456 Squadron aircraft). Joe (Blue 1) is overall formation leader, Flying Officer J. E. Wootton with Pilot Officer J. M. Dymock are Blue 2 and Cheney/Mycock are Blue 3. Flight Lieutenant Panitz is Green 1 (navigator unknown) and Newell/Keating, Richardson/Landy are Green 2 and 3 respectively.

Taking off at 1430hrs, the formation flies in two Vics[6] in loose line astern. Half an hour after take-off, Green 1 (Panitz) reports engine trouble and returns to base. Joe instructs Green 2 and 3 to re-position themselves as Blue 4 and 5, creating one large formation. At about 1615, with the formation flying at 50 ft, Blue 2 (Wootton) sights a formation of five Ju 88s at a height of around 5,000 ft.[7] Ordering them to close up in the climb, Joe manoeuvres his formation through scattered cloud, up-sun of the enemy aircraft. The Junkers indicate they have spotted the formation by starting a climb in loose line astern, firing three red star cartridges.

At about 5,500 ft, Joe orders his formation to split and attack; he selects the rearmost Ju 88, which is closest to him. Three or four of the enemy aircraft then open fire on him from their dorsal gun turrets, but the tracers are seen to pass well above him. Whilst turning inside his quarry, Joe opens fire at full deflection[8] with a burst of less than one second from about 800 yards, with cannon only, having discovered at that moment that his machine guns have failed (later diagnosed as an electrical fault). The enemy's port engine is seen to belch thick black smoke and he is seen to peel off to starboard in a dive. Joe follows him closely and gives him a second burst, now from dead astern, at about 300 yards' range, again of about a second's duration; sheets of flame are seen from outboard of the Ju 88's port engine; he is still returning fire to no effect. The enemy aircraft then pulls out of the dive. Joe is able to close to within 25 yards, give a three-second burst from dead astern causing more flames to appear inboard of the port engine, quickly followed by thick black smoke from his starboard. This covers Joe's windscreen with oil, compelling him to peel off rapidly to starboard to avoid a collision. Regaining some vision, Joe follows the Junkers into a steep dive and, from above, at an angle of about 45 degrees, fires the fourth and final burst, whereupon pieces of the engine cowling and mainplane fly off.

Joe and Geoff watch as two crewmembers of the Ju 88 bail out from the top hatch, one of whom hits the tailplane. Their stricken aircraft rolls into a vertical dive from 2,000 ft and hits the sea. All the remaining enemy having now disappeared and being short of fuel, Joe orders his scattered formation to return independently. However, he has the presence of mind to take a photo of the oil patch left by his

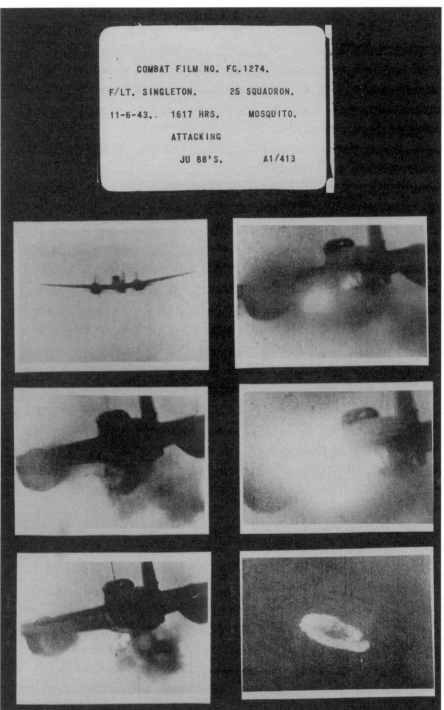

COMBAT FILM NO. FC.1274.

F/LT. SINGLETON.   25 SQUADRON.

11-6-43.. 1617 HRS.   MOSQUITO.

ATTACKING

JU 88'S.   A1/413

Junkers. The crew of this Ju 88 – Fritz Hiebsch (pilot), Peter Hoffman (observer) and Erwin Seidel (radio operator) – were all killed.[9] During the engagement, Wootton claims another 'Damaged' and Newell two others. With all his formation landing safely, Joe's logbook entry reads:

MET 5 JU 88S AND ATTACKED – 1 JU 88 DESTROYED.

In due course, stills from his gun-camera footage (see opposite) were released and Joe's local papers duly made a fuss of their new hero.

Joe flew down to Predannack in Mosquito DZ 685 and he flew his two Instep Patrols in that airframe. His logbook records him returning to Church Fenton on the day following this last patrol, also in DZ 685. But, according to the 25 Squadron ORB, he is mistaken. It records for Saturday 12th June:

> *This afternoon F/Lt J. Singleton and F/O W. G. Haslam returned in Mosquito II DD757 from their detachment at Predannack and received a great welcome as a result of their successes … F/Lt A. S. H Baillie with his Navigator P/O D. C. Burrow were ferried to Hornchurch and proceeded from there in Mosquito II DD 738 to Predannack to act as replacement crew on detachment to 264 Squadron.*

Normally, such a minor logbook inaccuracy would be overlooked, but this one is remarkable because it is yet another example of the twists of fate and fortune experienced by Joe. 25 Squadron's Aircraft Disposals List shows an entry, which substantiates the slip-up as follows:

DZ 685 Destroyed by Focke-Wulf, Fw 190, 13/6/43.

DZ 685 could not have been destroyed by a Fw 190 if it had been at Church Fenton, as the latter simply did not have the range to be encountered that far north. So, having been recalled early from the detachment, Joe left DZ 685 at Predannack for another 25 Squadron crew to fly – believed to be Wootton – and flew another of their aircraft home. One wonders if the recipient felt fortunate to be taking over Joe's aircraft, since it had just carried him to successes on its two previous Insteps.

MILE-HIGH KILL OVER BISCAY ✕

IN an air battle which began at 6,500 feet over the Bay of Biscay three Mosquitoes, which had climbed from sea level to attack five Junkers 88's, shot one down, damaged three, and returned safely.

Twenty-seven-year-old Flight-Lieutenant Joseph Singleton, of Leyland (Lancashire), who led the Mosquitoes, got the only "kill," and saw the Junkers crash into the sea.

"We caught them at 6,500 feet," he said, "and I told the boys to pick Huns for themselves. I chose one myself and gave it a short burst from long range.

"He was hit in the port engine, and I gave him another burst which set his engine on fire. At 25 yards I gave him another, setting his other engine on fire.

"Two parachutes billowed out, and the Junkers went into the sea."

Flight-Lieutenant Singleton led a troop of Boy Scouts before joining up two days after war started.

He turned down a rest period to help fight the battle of the Atlantic.

A Mosquito of Fighter Command destroyed a twin-engined enemy plane as it was landing at its base in Holland. It blew up on the runway.

LEYLAND LEADER OF DARING MOSQUITOS

Flight-Lieut. Joseph Singleton (27), leader of three Mosquitos which took on five JU 88s over the Bay of Biscay, destroying one and damaging three others is the only son of Mr. and Mrs. A. Singleton, of 160, Golden Hill-lane, Leyland, who read of his exploit in the newspapers. He recently returned from leave. Flt.-Lieut. Singleton who volunteered on the Wednesday following outbreak of war, was manager of advertising and printing at Leyland Paint and Varnish

LEYLAND MAN LED MOSQUITOS IN BAY OF BISCAY BATTLE

FLIGHT LIEUTENANT J SINGLETON, of Leyland led three Mosquitos, of Fighter Command which fought five Junkers 88s in a Bay of Biscay air battle on Friday of last week states the Air Ministry News Service. After destroying one of the enemy aircraft and damaging three others all the Mosquitos returned safely.

Singleton's No 2, a flying officer from North London, who is 23, damaged one and the other two were damaged by an Australian pilot officer, who was 26 on the previous Tuesday.

The Mosquitos were flying at less than 100 feet above the sea when the flying officer reported five enemy aircraft about 5,000 feet above them.

LEADER'S STORY

"I gave the boys instructions to climb," said the flight lieutenant on his return.

"We caught them at about 6,500 feet and then I said, 'O.K., boys. All take a Hun for yourselves.'

"I picked out one and gave it a short burst from long range. It was hit in the port engine and smoke began to pour out of it. He peeled off to starboard, and I followed him down and gave him another burst from astern, which started flames in his port engine.

"I closed to within 25 yards and gave him a third burst, setting his other engine on fire. We were down to about 1,600 feet when two parachutes billowed out of the 'plane and opened up. The Junker carried on into the sea."

Flight Lieut. Singleton, who is 27, is the only son of Mr. and Mrs. A. Singleton, of 160, Golden Hill-lane, Leyland. He volunteered on the Wednesday following the outbreak of war. He was then manager of advertising and print-

Heavy Blows

Mosquito Destroys Ju.88 Over Bay Of Biscay

Three Mosquitos of R.A.F. Fighter Command sighted five Ju. 88s over the Bay of Biscay. The Mosquitos, led by a flight-lieutenant from Golden Hill Lane, Leyland, Lancashire, climbed to engage them. "Take a Hun each, boys," called the flight-lieutenant over the radio telephone, and this series of photographs, taken from the cine-film record of his own combat, shows how he dealt with his own selected victim, from the "sighting" to the funeral "wreath."

All Singleton Private Collection.

And Out Goes He!

WHEN over the Bay of Biscay a Flight-Lieutenant from Golden Hill Lane, Leyland, Lancs, got this Ju 88 lined up in his gun sights. He pressed the button, and the second picture shows the first strikes getting home. Closing in he set the port engine and wing ablaze from 25 yards range (third picture). "He peeled off to starboard," said the Flight Lieutenant, and two parachutes billowed out of the aircraft."

The Ju. crumpled and hit the sea, and all that was presently left of it was the "wreath" of foam marking the grave of yet another Hun aircraft.

Regardless, according to the ORB, on Sunday 13th June, four Mosquitos – Cheney, Wootton and a Pilot Officer R. B. Harris of 410 Squadron, with respective navigators and with Baillie now leading, took off from Predannack at 1259 hrs. During the patrol, four Ju 88s were sighted at 7,000 ft and Baillie called the attack. On spotting their pursuers, the Germans broke formation and climbed into a layer of cloud. Baillie lost sight of both them and his colleagues until, on emerging from the cloud layer, he saw his formation at sea level, well ahead. He was unable to catch up to join them and soon lost them altogether; he returned to base and landed at 1750 hrs (an exceptionally long sortie – he must have been very low on fuel). Between 1710 hrs and 1725 hrs Flight Officer Wootton radioed for an emergency homing to Predannack and a further message from one of the aircraft stated that they were being chased by Fw 190s. Not one of these three aircraft returned to base and nothing is known of their fate. The ORB concludes eloquently:

> *It would, however, seem that there is little hope of their survival, and the Squadron must necessarily face the loss of two very capable crews, and four officers for whom we hold a high regard.*

Chris Goss identifies the attacking FW 190s as two aircraft of Jagdgeschwader 2 piloted by Oberfeldwebel (Warrant Officer) Fritz May and Feldwebel (Flight Sergeant) Alois Schnoll. Flying out of Brest and supporting U-boat operations, May shot down two and Schnoll one of the Mosquitos.

To lead a formation on an unfamiliar operation, within 24 hours of his arrival, is indeed a very high expectation, by both Baillie himself and of Baillie by his superiors. The effect on the man of losing the six young men in his formation, can only be guessed at. That he must have almost run out of fuel, before he landed and faced the reality, could be one indicator that he was desperate not to abandon them. But it cannot be mere coincidence that Alastair Stuart Hamilton Baillie, exactly one year later, on 13th June 1944, flying 25 Squadron Mosquito XVII HK 288, was posted as missing from an Intruder Operation over the Netherlands. He is buried in Brummen, Netherlands, not far from Twente, site of Joe's Intruders the previous month. His gravestone reads:

FLIGHT LIEUTENANT
A. S. H. BAILLIE
PILOT
ROYAL AIR FORCE
13TH JUNE 1994 AGE 30

He was the son of Stuart Fraser and Andrewina Baillie, of Moidart, Renfrewshire; he was the husband of Anne Baillie.

Flying Officer Jack Cheney was one of the new pilots Joe had given instruction to when he first arrived on the Squadron, earlier in the year. Cheney's first flight in a Mosquito was with Joe in DZ 688 on 4th Feb 1943; it is, almost certainly, also the aircraft in which he died. A typical Jack-the-Lad young fighter pilot, Cheney nevertheless was in the habit of keeping a diary of his wartime life, up to shortly before his detachment to Predannack. Alastair Goodrum developed the diary into a three-part serialisation for Flypast Magazine in late 1988. Joe was asked by Goodrum to proofread and correct the extract, which follows Cheney's arrival on 25 Squadron in January 1943. An extract from the proof, with Joe's comments, covering Jack Cheney's first meeting with the Mosquito and Joe is in the Appendix. It provides a fascinating insight into Cheney's experiences, attitudes, triumphs and frustrations. According to Goodrum, Luftwaffe diaries record that on the day following the losses (14th June), General Adolph Galland reported personally to Hitler that a force of Mosquitos had been engaged over the Bay of Biscay and four [sic] of them had been shot down. The Fw 190s were most likely from Jagdkommando Brest – a small flight of six aircraft established to counteract the success achieved by the Instep crew (agreeing with Chris Goss).

There were two further ramifications of the events in Predannack. On 17th June, with the distinct sound of a stable door being bolted,

25 Squadron 16th June 1943. Singleton Private Collection.

25 Squadron set in place fighter affiliation exercises with local Spitfire squadrons:

> *This will afford valuable practice in day evasive and fighting tactics, and it is a direct result of the lessons learned and losses suffered during the Bay of Biscay engagement on the 13th June 1943.*

Notwithstanding, the Air Ministry did not miss the opportunity of glossing over those lessons and making available to the press (some two months later for obvious security reasons) the details and dramatic photos of Joe's contribution to the Battle for the Atlantic.

Joe was recalled to Church Fenton to be posted for 'a rest from operations'; whether or not he was aware of the plan before his departure for Predannack, is not clear but unlikely. A farewell party was thrown in the Officers' Mess at Church Fenton on the night of the

15th June and, the following day, the Station Commander – Group Captain F. W. Stannard – said a few farewell words, after which the 16th June 1943 25 Squadron photograph was taken. The squadron's ORB writer was moved to make the following entry:

> Today F/Lt J Singleton 69431 left the Squadron on posting to TFU Defford … We thus lose, perhaps, only for a while, [one] of the Squadron's most capable and experienced members. F/Lt Singleton, or Joe Singleton as he is always known, completes a tour of duty characterised by great keenness and unselfish devotion to duty, and marked with considerable success. He has, while with the Squadron, won two confirmed victories and damaged, or probably destroyed, four more enemy aircraft, besides carrying out several successful Ranger sorties by night. It is our firm hope and [his] avowed intention that [he] will return to the Squadron before many months.

The sheer weight of numbers of victims of 'shell-shock' in WWI, fostering extensive research between the wars, had convinced most of the military and medical hierarchy in Britain that combat stress was a condition to be managed, rather than denied. Experience from the Battle of Britain and the early days of the Bomber Offensive had led to the RAF introducing and enacting, from 1941, the concept of a finite 'Tour of Duty' for front-line aircrew, to limit their exposure to trauma and exhaustion. The duration varied according to the type of operations to which the aircrew was exposed. For Bomber Command crews the indicator was 30 operational sorties, i.e. over enemy territory with confirmation their bombs were dropped on the target area (usually by photograph). For Coastal Command, whose sorties tended to be a lot longer but with less opposition, used the guideline of whichever came first: 800 hours or 18 months. Single seat fighter tours, certainly in the early part of the war, varied considerably depending on location. As a rule of thumb, the nearer to London, the more scrambles and engagements, the shorter the tours. But this became complicated by Fighter Command's policy of regularly rotating squadrons into, and out of, the hot spots of southern England. Tour lengths thus became a matter for the squadron commander to make a judgment. He was given the responsibility to monitor each of his pilots for signs that they were in need of a rest. Stories are legion of fighter pilots avoiding giving the Boss any reason to think they might be in need of rest. There were also those squadron commanders who did not go along with the theory that combat stress was anything other than 'Lack of Moral Fibre'.

The Mosquito was something of a hybrid in this regard. Their duties were rarely in the pressure cooker of southern England and there were long periods of inactivity. But night flying, even without fighting, brought its own unique stresses and, latterly, daytime operations such as Instep Patrols were being thrown into the mix. A night fighter squadron commander had to take all this into account. The general guideline for Mosquito squadrons was 200 intensive hours flying. By any benchmark Joe was long overdue an operational rest. But for short breaks, for courses and leave, he had been continuously on 25 Squadron since November 1941 – just over 18 months. He had flown almost 400 hours by day and over 200 hours by night, divided roughly in half between Beaufighters and Mosquitos. The three squadron commanders under whom he had served during that time – H. P. Pleasance, E. G. Watkins and J. L. Shaw – would have been fully aware that Joe was, increasingly, an asset the Squadron could ill afford to lose. He was an exceptional pilot, a successful night fighter, flying instructor and role model for the youngsters and possessed that priceless attribute – luck. But enough is enough. Even though there is no evidence that Joe was showing any kind of strain – judging by his Predannack exploits, quite the opposite – Wing Commander J. L. Shaw had decided that Joe needed a break. So, with evident reluctance and leaving Geoff Haslam behind, Joe departed for RAF Defford, vowing to return. He left 25 Squadron assessed as 'Exceptional' as a night-fighter pilot and pilot navigator, 'Above Average' as an Air Gunner. Could Joe have been a little miffed with not getting 'Exceptional' as an Air Gunner?

Postscript to Predannack Interlude

In the whole war, before May 1943, Coastal Command had sighted submarines on 825 occasions, which resulted in 607 attacks. Only 27 were reported as 'sunk', and three were shared 'destroyed'; another 120 were 'damaged'. Against those figures, 233 aircraft, 116 of which were lost owing to weather conditions, were destroyed. Of this figure, 179 were from 19 Group, attacking U-boats over the Bay of Biscay.

Changes in convoy techniques and revised command structures to co-ordinate naval and unify air effort, particularly between the Canadian and British, began to show significant benefits by May 1943. In addition, the newly introduced long-range Liberators, based in

Departure for Defford. Singleton Private Collection.

Newfoundland and Iceland had closed the 'air gap' (a sizeable portion of the convoys' route, beyond the range of aircraft emanating from either east or west that could provide defence against U-boats) in the North Atlantic. During the year 1943, U-boat losses amounted to 258 to all causes. Of this total, Coastal Command sank 90, with 51 damaged.

The defeat of the U-boats in the mid-Atlantic, and their withdrawal, meant the Bay of Biscay became congested with German submarines seeking refuge. Consequently, Air Marshal Sir John Slessor, Commander-in-Chief Coastal Command revisited the interdiction strategy, which had been tried and failed in 1941 and 1942. This time, there were crucial differences. Firstly, the improvement of radar had enhanced detection of submarines, submerged and surfaced. Second were the intelligence breakthroughs. The British Ultra organisation had broken the German Navy's Enigma codes and confirmed a major change in strategy – away from the Mid Atlantic Gap. This enabled the British to focus on the Bay of Biscay. When renewed air operations began over the Bay, the Command found U-boats not only adhering to this new strategy (of avoidance); they discovered the Germans obeying new tactical instructions. The German crews were ordered to transit the Bay in groups, submerged at night, but on the surface in daylight, to concentrate their defensive fire. Later U-boat designs had their firepower upgraded for this purpose. Also, the Luftwaffe provided night fighters to escort the submarines. The increased firepower and determination of German air and submarine crews to fight it out did not deter British crews. The Third Bay Offensive became the bloodiest in the air-submarine battle yet, which involved heavy losses. Despite strenuous German efforts to defend themselves, by 17 June, air attacks had forced German submarines to make the trip submerged during daylight. The effects were not just indirect; Coastal Command patrols inflicted increasing losses on German U-boats. From 1st July to 2nd August 1943, 86 submarines passed through the Bay, 55 were sighted and 16 sunk, in exchange for 14 aircraft.

9.

An Exhausting Rest

(16th June–29th December 1943)

Telecommunications Flying Unit (TFU), RAF Defford

In 1935, as a result of Sir Henry Tizard's Committee producing a Scientific Survey of Air Defence, four 'Men of Vision' – A. P. Rowe, H. E. Wimperis, A. F. Wilkins and Robert Watson-Watt – all scientists working in the field of radio waves, were brought together and given an initial one million pounds for their research. The fusion of the knowledge and genius of these four and their teams was the catalyst for remarkable innovation. The early outputs were the Chain Home and Chain Home (Low) to detect incoming raids, and the Ground Controlled Interception (GCI) radars to enable fighters to find their targets. The initial group of 'boffins' were put at Orfordness near Ipswich, moving to Bawdsey Research Station, near Felixstowe in 1936 – both sited near the coast to facilitate experimentation of radar over water, without ground clutter. It was there that one of Watson-Watt's protégés – Dr Eddie 'Taffy' Bowen – was given the job of leading the team looking into airborne radar. Within a few days of the outbreak of war, however, it was belatedly realised how vulnerable Bawdsey was to air attack from Germany. Watson-Watt, who had worked there previously, arranged for the entire team to rapidly de-camp to Dundee University's research facilities. It was there that the team working on equipment destined for the RAF were christened the Air Ministry Research Establishment (AMRE), under the directorship of A. P. Rowe. Bowen's sub-team working on the airborne radar, however, found the facilities less than adequate. Bowen also did not see eye-to-eye with the autocratic Rowe, who had no confidence that radars could be sufficiently miniaturised, to be carried in aircraft, in the required timescale. Rowe believed that technology was 'for the next war'. Bowen then made another unsuccessful move to St Athan near Swansea before re-joining the team in May 1940, when they moved to Worth Matravers, near Swanage on the south coast. AMRE's aircraft flew Bowen's AI products from RAF Christchurch. In November 1940, Rowe's whole team were re-named the Telecommunications Research Establishment (TRE) and its Christchurch trials aircraft unit the Telecommunications Flying Unit (TFU). Over the winter of 1941–2, it became increasingly obvious to TRE that the success rate of fighters against the Combined Bomber Offensive was a sure sign of a technical breakthrough the Germans had made with their radars. Using their now considerable influence in the corridors of power, they persuaded Louis Mountbatten[1] to initiate a daring and very successful raid on a radar station at Bruneval, in occupied France, on the night of 27th/28th February 1942. One of the raiding party was a TRE scientist and, for relatively few casualties, vital components of the Wurzburg radar were captured, along with two German radar technicians, providing vital information. Just one of the fruits of that raid, destined to save countless bomber crews' lives, was the widespread introduction of Window[2] into RAF aircraft to confuse enemy radars. A few weeks later, the press made a meal of the glamorous action – a heaven-sent ray of light in the extant gloom.

Before that, however, it was realised that, if German secrets could be stolen that way, then reciprocation was entirely possible. A significant reason for the success of the raid had been Bruneval's proximity to the coast; so the south coast of England was just about the worst place for TRE to be located. Churchill himself ordered this precious national top-secret organisation moved, forthwith, further away from danger. Malvern College, a public school in Worcestershire (close to the Army-oriented radar research team), was requisitioned and the move made in May 1942. Consequently, the TFU, also near the coast at Christchurch, immediately had to follow to continue the vital flight trials. There was spare capacity at a satellite of RAF Pershore – RAF Defford – some 12 miles from Malvern. The need to keep the TFU adjacent to TRE, with no interruption, over-rode the fact that there was almost no accommodation to house what was, by now, a major flying organisation. 'Move aircraft and pitch tents' was the order of the day. With over 1,000 staff moving to Malvern alone, it was imperative that more permanent accommodation was built. Corrugated iron was the material of choice.

Nevertheless, TRE had the imposing Victorian school buildings to use as a base (the school had been given a week's notice to vacate, moving to share the facilities at Harrow School). Similar solutions were rapidly put in place at Defford, but the TFU had an equally impressive new headquarters in the requisitioned Croome Court, built in the 18th century by the sixth Earl of Coventry. The landscaping by Lancelot Capability Brown and the house interior by Robert Adam were, no doubt, much appreciated the TFU.

By the time Joe arrived at Defford, over a year after the move from Christchurch, the TFU was nearing its peak of 100 aircraft and 2,000 personnel, all now housed in (semi-)permanent living accommodation, with an Officers' Mess erected just inside the main gates, as well as the Court itself. There would be no tents for Joe!

The TFU provided the airborne test-beds for the ideas, experiments and equipment emerging from the Telecommunications Research Establishment. Having been at the point of the spear for eighteen months, Joe was about to discover how the spear and shaft were designed and made. TRE were working on: offensive and defensive bomber, fighter and anti-submarine/surface vessel radars; radio navigation aids; precision approach aids; and the radar jamming/anti-jamming capabilities. All of this work was classified at least 'Secret', much of it 'Top Secret'. As captain of a trials aircraft, Joe would be told only as much as was necessary for him to facilitate that particular trial. Often that would mean lengthy classified briefings with TRE to ensure he knew how to get the maximum out of each trial. If, for instance, it was a new development in AI being tested, with his long experience of night fighting, he would be able to significantly contribute practical knowledge to the trial. There would be times, however, when he would fly with military technicians and/or civilian boffins, in the back of his aircraft with their equipment, and have little or no idea what they were up to. If he could fulfil his role without knowing, the secrecy principle of 'need-to-know' ruled him out of being told.

Most of Joe's logbook entries for this period are suitably cryptic. Most simply appear as 'ITEM X', X being a variety of numbers referring to different trials, using particular aircraft, within a schedule pre-agreed between TRE and TFU. There are also code words, such as 'SLEDGE GREEN', which happens to be the name of a small village a few miles to the south of Malvern. Presumably these describe a particular activity, such as a run against one of TRE's static radars. One can imagine a typical telephone conversation between a boffin at Malvern and the Ops desk at Defford, to set up the next day's trial, intended to mislead an eavesdropper into thinking it could be a delivery company:

> OK, tomorrow we've got an Item 10, two Item 43s and an Item 115 at Sledge Green. We'll drop off [deliver and fit the equipment] tomorrow morning, ready for pick-up [flight trial] in the afternoon.

Much of Joe's activities at Defford are shrouded in mystery. What can be gleaned from his logbook, and deduced from known TRE activity at that time, is that it is highly likely that Joe worked on the following:

1. The Mk VIII AI, the British centimetric AI already coming into service in night fighters, but on which work was still required to iron out the worst imperfections.[3] Mosquito NF IIs converted to

take the AI Mk VIII were designated Mosquito Mk XII, as Joe would know when he returned to 25 Squadron.

2. The Mk 10 (or X) AI, the US development of the centimetric AI, which had been recently supplied by the Americans and was being worked on. It would soon be fitted onto on Mosquitos designated the Mk XVII and become the mainstay of RAF AI for the remainder of the war.

3. On 24th July 1943, around one month after Joe's arrival at Defford, the devastating attack on Hamburg, and subsequent fire storm, had used Window very effectively to jam enemy radars. TRE were now working on counter-measures to the German equivalent – Duppel.

4. TRE had conceived the radio navigation aids GEE and OBOE which had been in service for some time, providing much greater accuracy for Bomber Command, both of which were constantly being refined. Another system – H2S, using ground radar returns for navigation and bomb release was also being developed. These technologies would be utilised for many years to come.

5. Joe had been using BABS (either Beam or Blind Approach Beacon System depending on source)[4] for some time, but it was being refined all the time.[5] It was widely recognised as significantly reducing attrition of aircraft and crews due to accidents as they tried to land at night and/or in bad weather (e.g. fog or low cloud). As a matter of routine, pilots were now being sent on week-long courses (Joe would complete his at the end of October 1943), to familiarise themselves with this difficult-to-master but invaluable aid.

For Joe, his 'rest from operations' at Defford did not mean a rest from flying. He was flying at almost the same rate of sorties per day as he had been on the squadron. Generally, the sorties were significantly shorter – there was no hanging around waiting for trade – but they would each have packed in as much data gathering for the boffins as possible, and so had an intensity of their own. He was, however, able to take more leave and in longer chunks than he had been able (or inclined) to for a long time. Aside from a few days between Church Fenton and Defford, he was presented with the luxury of a two-week break at the beginning of September 1943.

This 'coincided' with the promulgation, in the *London Gazette* on 3rd September, of the award of his Distinguished Flying Cross (see citation below). He would have been told some time before (probably many weeks and perhaps by the CO before leaving 25 Squadron), that it was in the pipeline. But, in accordance with tradition, it was not official and so it could not be celebrated, until it had been 'Gazetted'. It is more than likely that OC TFU readily granted him leave to go and share the honour with family and friends. It would be surprising if a sherry with Mum and Dad in Leyland, and a beer or two with Geoff Haslam and the boys of 25 Squadron, were not included in that mix, during the fortnight.

Distinguished Flying Cross

London Gazette 3rd September, 1943

Acting Flight Lieutenant Joseph SINGLETON, Royal Air Force Volunteer Reserve, No. 25 Squadron.

Flight Lieutenant Singleton has served with his present squadron for 18 months and latterly became a flight commander. His work has been of a very high standard and his efficiency, an example to all air crews. During night defence patrols he has destroyed 1 and damaged several enemy aircraft and while on a sweep in the Bay of Biscay he destroyed a Junkers 88. His sorties over Germany and occupied territory have resulted in damage and destruction to many locomotives.

DFC citation, London Gazette. *Singleton Private Collection.*

In addition, he was beginning to become known to a wider audience. Local papers around Leyland had already run minor stories in the aftermath of his Bay of Biscay exploits. When his DFC appeared in the *Gazette*, the same papers re-ran the story, as did papers around Fort Augustus, along the lines of 'Abbey School Old Boy a Hero'.

During his six months with the TFU at Defford, in addition to Beaufighters and Mosquito which were the mainstays, Joe flew in eight different aircraft types,: Hurricane, Havoc, Spitfire, Miles Mentor, Wellington, Oxford, Boston and, curiously, the Swordfish. Naval

Singleton Private Collection.

Joe and Geoff Halsam reunited, Acklington January 1944. Joe's banger still survives.
Singleton Private Correction.

pilots and support personnel were an integral part of the TFU. Their main role was to test-fly the Anti-Surface Vessel radars, which did so much to enable the Royal Navy and Coastal Command to win the Battle of the Atlantic and (eventually) the U-Boat War. It seems that the RN pilots had brought with them a Swordfish, for trials or as a 'hack', or both. On 2nd November, Joe persuaded them to let him have a go with this biplane, made famous by wreaking havoc amongst the Italian Navy's capital ships in Taranto Harbour, almost exactly two years previously. He flies for one hour with a Wren Able Seaman who is nameless (perhaps he forgot to ask her…), in the rear seat. He obviously enjoyed the experience, recording:

S.I.U.[6] TEST – S.F. FLIES LIKE A GLORIFIED TIGER.

The assumption is that 'S.F.' refers to the Swordfish and not to the Wren. Whatever her name, she probably never knew what a lucky woman she was. Later in his life, Joe many times told the story that during this sortie, realising just how 'glorified' the Swordfish was, he tried to persuade the Wren to let him do some aerobatics – maybe a loop, a slow roll perhaps. But, disappointingly for Joe, she was adamant that just flying the right way up was sufficient for her! On landing, he got out first and gallantly helped her out of the rear cockpit – whereupon he realised to his horror that she had never been strapped in.[7] If she had agreed to his exhortations for aerobatics, any negative g-force could well have caused her to vacate the open cockpit of the aircraft prematurely.

By the time he was signed off in his logbook as 'Exceptional' by OC of the TFU, W/Cdr J C Claydon, on 28th December 1943, Joe had flown a total of 184 hours with the TFU, most of which was on the Beaufighter (94 hrs) and the Mosquito (48 hrs). Having got his wish to return to 25 Squadron, which he does on paper from 30th December 1943, Joe is unlikely to have missed the opportunity to make the New Year's celebrations also his homecoming.

10.

Three in Thirteen

(30th December 1943–20th March 1944)

25 Squadron, RAF Acklington

(30th December 1943–5th February 1944)

On arrival at Acklington to take the post of 'A' Flight Commander, Joe finds that 25 Squadron has moved on. The Commanding Officer is now Wing Commander Cathcart M. Wight-Boycott and the squadron has moved from Church Fenton to RAF Acklington in Northumberland. During his absence, ten squadron aircraft and crews have been lost, half to accidents and half due to enemy action, mainly whilst on Intruder operations. So there are a lot of faces Joe does not recognise and a lot of friends absent; but Geoff Haslam is still there and they look pretty pleased to be re-united.

Indeed, there are only five faces on the 28th February 1944 photograph that also appear on that from June 1943. Another prominent difference between the two photos is the presence on the latter of four Royal Navy officers, presaging a new air/sea role Joe was soon to adopt. The Squadron has just (December 43) taken delivery of the first batch of five Mosquito XVIIs fitted with the latest AI Mk X, supplied by the US and worked on by TRE, with its 'thimble' radome in place of the four machine guns in the nose. No doubt Joe was able to throw some light on this new wonder, from his experiences at Defford. The Squadron is to receive thirteen more Mosquito XVIIs before the end of January, and a total of 26 by September 1944, when the Mosquito 30[1] start arriving. Whilst re-equipping with these new aircraft, Intruder and Ranger operations are being wound down, although one of the remaining NFIIs is written off in an accident at Acklington on returning from an Intruder, a week after Joe arrived there; the crew survive.

Acklington is also home to another Mosquito squadron[2] – 410 RCAF and, compared to Church Fenton, the accommodation is rather rudimentary, consisting largely of pre-fabricated metal Nissen (arched) and wooden Uni-Seco (pitched) huts.[3] The Type 2 hangars are large metal and asbestos structures capable of housing about eight Mosquitos and the airfield has three concrete runways.

On 3rd January, accompanied by Geoff H., Joe gets down to the business of re-acquainting himself with squadron operations, with a Night Flying Test sortie in a Mosquito. The rest of the month, aside from a drogue-towing trip in a Miles Martinet with Geoff, is taken up with interception practice with the local GCIs and some air-to-surface firing practice. On 23rd January, they carry out their first night patrol together in Mosquito Mk XVII 255, which becomes their own machine for some time to come; three more patrols are carried out in January. Joe has indeed returned to 25 Squadron at a most propitious moment: offensive operations on the back burner, the most capable night fighter of its day at his disposal and plenty of 'trade' coming his way. Not only that, things are about to get even more exciting because, just a month after arriving at Acklington, the Squadron is on the move again and this time much closer to Germany and the action – Norfolk. Men and machines are moved and operational again in less than a week (last sortie from Acklington 31st January, first from Coltishall 7th February) – a remarkable achievement and testament to the logistic capabilities of the RAF at a critical moment in the war.

25 Squadron, RAF Coltishall

(5th February–17th May 1944)

They now have to rapidly get to know their local GCI and CH (L) – Neatishead and Happisburgh[4] also both in Norfolk. But first their naval connections take centre stage. The first indication that AI X has also been adapted (by TRE/TFU) to provide the capability to detect objects on the surface of the sea, comes on the 8th February:

A.S. RESCUE SEARCH FOR TYPHOON.

This capability not only has the obvious application of anti-surface vessel (ASV) warfare (as Joe demonstrated at Predannack), but also to cut down British losses of aircrew who bale out over the sea. Death from exposure could happen in a matter of minutes in winter, but survival times were much longer if the aircrew could get into the dinghy attached to their parachute pack. It was critical, therefore, that GCIs who watched (and possibly heard) a bale-out or ditching on their screens, could quickly scramble Mosquitos with this capability and direct them to the search area. Having located survivors, the Mosquito would then contact shipping in the locality to direct a pick up – this is where the RN personnel on the Squadron would come in handy, by facilitating the ship to aircraft link. On this occasion, however, Joe and Geoff draw a blank.

In late 1943, Hitler had ordered the Luftwaffe to mount another bomber offensive – Operation *Steinbock* – against southern England, in particular London. He was not to know (nor would he have accepted) that this was to be the last throw of the dice for the German bombers. Due to attrition on the Eastern Front, constant Intruder interference, and mounting supply problems, Goering could not muster any more than 500 bombers for the entire operation. For any one raid the

Booted and spurred: Joe and Geoff Haslam RAF Coltishall(?) 1944.
Singleton Private Collection.

numbers started at about 400 in January and dwindled to no more than 100 by the time the operation was called off in mid-May. The three-month period of increased enemy air activity over England (January–March 1944) became known as the Little, or Baby Blitz. Compared with the Night Blitz of three years earlier, when the RAF's night capability was negligible, this was a much better prospect for the night fighter squadrons which were prepared and numerous. By the end of the Baby Blitz, Goering would have fewer than 100 bombers left to attack Britain, until replenishments started to trickle in again.

Joe and Geoff are soon in the thick of the action. They are scrambled on both the 11th and 12th, and mount another routine patrol on 15th February. Then on the night of the 20th, they are scrambled at 2110 hrs, contact Neatishead GCI who give instructions to climb to

25 Squadron RAF Coltishall, 28th February 1944. Joe second from left, back row; Geoff in cockpit with 'Popski' the dog. Alastair Baillie second man to Geoff's left. Singleton Private Collection.

Angels 18 (18,000 ft) and patrol over East Anglia. Half an hour later they are handed over to the control of Flight Lieutenant Brodie at Happisburgh CH(L). After two fruitless chases, Brodie reports a bogey heading east, below them at Angels 10. Joe gives chase out over the North Sea and, at 2228 hrs, Geoff reports a gently weaving contact on his AI at range three miles, 30 degrees to starboard at 9,000 ft. Having manoeuvred to silhouette the bogey against a layer of cloud, and closing to a range of around 1,000 ft, Geoff identifies the aircraft as a Do 217 using night binoculars,[5] which Joe confirms at range 200 yards with his eyeball Mk 1.

A two-second burst of canon from dead astern produces fireworks on the Dornier's port wing and engine, whereupon it immediately climbs 1,000 ft, turning to port. Closing in again is no problem due to the bright trail of sparks and, from 100 yards, Joe gives another burst of 3.5 seconds, scoring strikes on the fuselage, port engine and wing root. A big explosion then occurs on the port side of the Dornier, which immediately causes it to plummet, blazing fiercely. Following him down, from about 3,000 ft, they see the Dornier hit the sea about 50 miles east of Lowestoft at 2236 hrs. Throughout, no return fire is seen from the Dornier. On gathering his thoughts, Geoff discovers his AI had been degraded by the engagement – 'weapon behaving badly'. Nevertheless, they call Brodie at Happisburgh who gives them another bogey to chase which they do for about 15–20 minutes until, being unable to catch up, they turn for home some 20 miles short of the Dutch coast. They land back at Coltishall at 2340 hrs. Joe's logbook records:

DORNIER 217 DESTROYED.

In his Combat Report, Joe comments on Flight Lieutenant Brodie's 'excellent controlling'; and records they expended 120 of each of High Explosive Incendiary (HEI) and Semi-Amour Piercing Incendiary (SAPI) 20mm cannon rounds. 25 Squadron's ORB catches the uplift in morale the night of 20th/21st February causes:

A red letter day for the squadron's 'A' Flight. [Joe is Flight Commander] Indications of trade were received at about 1930 hours, and shortly after four crews were scrambled, amongst them being P/O Brockbank with P/O McCausland, and F/ Lt Singleton with F/O Haslam...[Brockbank and McCausland shoot down a Ju 188] ... this was the first confirmed victim for the Mk X [AI] ... [He then describes the Joe/GH shoot-down] Both of these crews ... did a splendid job, and it has put new life in the whole Squadron to see some return for a good deal of hard practice work.

Joe and Geoff are scrambled twice more during February (22nd and 24th), without results. Prior to the 24th scramble, whilst carrying out the usual day NFT, they are obviously asked to go and look for signs of downed aircrew:

AIR SEA RESCUE SEARCH. 2 DINGHIES FOUND.

Not good news for the crew. On the 28th there is a cryptic red-ink entry: '*EXERCISE WHITING.*' which smacks of practice liaison with the Royal Navy, but cannot be verified. So in the first three weeks based at Coltishall, Joe and Geoff have flown relatively little in terms of hours – around 30 – but they have seen plenty of action, with five scrambles and a confirmed kill, their fourth overall.

March 1944 begins rather quietly. It seems their aircraft HK 255 is out of commission for a few days and night flying is in short supply, perhaps for weather reasons, perhaps they were not on the night shifts. They do fit in a couple of land-aways to West Malling and Gravesend and a fruitless air-sea rescue search on the 7th. After a couple of air tests, 255 is readied for night flying on the 11th, which includes some co-operation with the Lowestoft and Yarmouth anti-aircraft gun crews. Sure enough, on the night of the 11th they are scrambled, but to no avail. Then, on the night of 14th March, Joe and Geoff get airborne at 2105 hrs, with three other 25 Squadron Mosquitos, to carry out a Bullseye Exercise[6] at the end of which, having plenty of fuel left, they call Neatishead GCI to ask if there is any trade; they are at Angels 18, it is 2210 hrs. Very shortly after being told there were 'possibilities', a contact appears on Geoff's AI scope heading straight towards them, slightly left of their nose, at a range of 4.5 miles. Neatishead give permission to follow the contact, but are unable to give any further assistance. Joe successfully carries out the standard manoeuvre to bring 255 onto the tail of the contact, which is flying at 16,000 ft and about 240 mph, in an orbit to starboard. At a range of 1,000 ft, Geoff uses the night vision binoculars to identify the aircraft as a Junkers 188 – an improved version of the Ju 88 with better performance and payload; it had, normally, a crew of five.

As he closes, Joe visually confirms the identification and, at a range of 75 yards, he gives it a three-second cannon burst from dead astern. There immediately is a big explosion in the port side of the fuselage (maybe he had hit their bombs) that sends the Ju 188 into a tight port turn and the German markings on the underside fill Joe's field of view, as he breaks hard the other way to avoid a collision. Joe follows him, now in a steep dive burning fiercely. At about 9,000 ft the Junkers breaks into two brightly burning portions that disappear into cloud at 5,000 ft. Shortly afterwards, a big explosion and blaze is seen reflected on the cloud cover, as it hits the sea. The three other Mosquitos have watched the whole episode unfold.

On landing at Coltishall just before midnight, Joe and Geoff get out to see slight debris damage to the leading edge of their starboard mainplane. Bearing in mind the mainly wooden construction, this proves once again that the Mosquito could withstand a remarkable amount of battle damage. Just 58 HEI and 58 SAPI rounds had brought the bomber down. They seem to be getting quite good at this and Joe's entry is simple:

JU 188 DESTROYED 3 MILES OFF SOUTHWOLD.

There is no resting on laurels, however, trade remains plentiful and the new Mosquito is obviously working very well for Joe and Geoff; they are airborne on patrol again the following night – Wednesday – but this time they draw a blank. Joe gives his HK 255 an air-test on the Thursday with LAC Henderson, one of his ground crew who had been with him for a long time (see photo June 1942 next to '"A" for Apple – Wizard Kite'), and then takes Friday off before a busy weekend on standby.

Joe flies on Saturday the 18th – a day trip with a Warrant Officer Ashton to check out the camera in 255. Sunday 19th March 1944 is a day that changes everything for Joe and Geoff. It was business as usual for the Spitfire Squadrons at Coltishall as they mounted various anti-shipping sweeps over the North Sea. In the afternoon, 25 Squadron carried out NFTs as usual, in preparation for the night flying programme and standby. Joe and Geoff in HK 255, along with Flight Lieutenant D. H. 'Douggie' Greaves[7] and Flying Officer

25 Squadron Aircrew on Standby, over a tense game of Uckers. Singleton Private Collection.

25 Sqn Aircrew on Standby at RAF Coltishall. Singleton Private Collection.

F. M. 'Charlie' Robbins (seen relaxing behind 25 Squadron's Dispersal in Joe's photo) as his navigator/radio operator in HK 278, are first and second on standby.

In the early evening, word comes through from 12 Group HQ[8] that something is afoot. At just before 2100 hrs, about 50 enemy aircraft are detected entering their area. Joe is scrambled at 2055 hrs, into a very dark but starlit night, rapidly followed by Greaves, who is operating independently. Heading east and having been urged to climb rapidly to 16,000 feet, Joe contacts Neatishead and then Happisburgh CH(L). He is turned more northerly and told twelve bandits are ahead, crossing from right to left. As advertised, Geoff picks up a contact at range 8.5 miles, coming from the right and at 15,000 feet. Joe manoeuvres onto the tail of the bogey and closes, whereupon both he and Geoff identify it as a Ju 188. At a range of 100 yards dead astern, Joe opens up with a 2.5-second burst of cannon. Strikes are scored on the fuselage, immediately followed by a big explosion. As with their previous encounter with a Ju 188 five days before, Joe is obliged to take rapid avoiding action (upwards) from pieces of the disintegrating target; but he gets spattered nevertheless. This time, however, there is no need to follow it. They orbit and watch, as it goes down in a steep diving turn to port, breaks up completely at about 5,000 feet and the burning pieces hit the sea, casting a glow over a wide area. It is 2120 hrs. Neatishead are able to give them a fix on the position of the kill – 56 miles NNE of Cromer– and they return to Happisburgh's radio frequency to see if they have any more trade.

They are told to head south and, almost immediately, Geoff picks up another contact on the AI, at range 4.5 miles, crossing slowly right to left. Again, Joe brings 255 into its 6 o'clock and, at range 1,500 feet, they both identify another Ju 188. Another 2.5-second burst from 100 yards causes a catastrophic explosion in the centre of the Junker's fuselage, which goes down almost vertically in flames and hits the sea, where the wreckage burns fiercely on the water. It is 2127 hrs. Orbiting, a fix from Neatishead establishes they are now 65 miles north-north-east of Cromer.

25 Sqn on Standby RAF Coltishall. Geoff Haslam on left. Singleton Private Collection.

Switching back to Happisburgh, still at 16,000 feet, there is no time for instructions before Geoff yells that he has another contact, at range four miles, crossing rapidly from right to left. A hard port turn brings Joe in behind this aircraft, which, unlike the previous two, is taking violent evasive action, up and down, left and right. They nevertheless identify it as yet another Ju 188, close to 125 yards astern and give it another 2.5 seconds of cannon rounds. Strikes are seen on the starboard engine, which emits large quantities of sparks and bursts into flames. With his prey losing height in a shallow dive, Joe tries a deflection shot from about 500–600 yards. Hits are scored and the Junkers becomes a mass of flames; bits of burning debris are seen to fly off, as it rapidly loses height and hits the sea, where it burns fiercely. It is 2133 hrs and they are at 14,000 ft, 80 miles north-north-east of Cromer;[9] but now they have problems. Joe's Combat Report Narrative says it all:

Annotated by Joe: Jimmie James, Johnny Linbent, Robbins, Brent Young, Bill Hamilton, Douggie Greaves, (?). Singleton Private Collection.

Immediately after combat I found my engines were running very rough and on examination, saw that the port Radiator Temperature Gauge was reading 140 degrees and the starboard about 120 degrees [both too high]. I throttled back, opened radiator flaps and got engines a little cooler. I told Happisburgh we were having engine trouble and was given a vector [direction for Coltishall] and told to go over to Neatishead. The port engine was emitting a lot of sparks and was very hot so I feathered it. Immediately the starboard engine overheated, so I unfeathered the port and flew with both engines throttled back as far as practicable, without too much loss of height. [Crossing the coast at about 5,000 feet] ... The radiator temperatures are reading 130–140 degrees ... I came through the funnels[10] at 1,000 feet ... At this point the starboard engine seized and burst into flames. I told Nav/Rad to operate the starboard engine fire extinguisher and I switched on the port landing light, since a crash looked inevitable and I was hoping it would help;[11] unfortunately it was not fully down when we landed. I tried to get more power out of the port engine, which, however, seized also. We got down into the red [too low] of the angle of glide, then the red disappeared [too low to register] and, with an ASI of 140 [mph], I levelled out a bit [with what speed he had left] and suddenly I felt the aircraft hit the ground. Nav/Rad [Geoff] opened the top hatch and jumped out, I followed a few seconds later and we got about 25 yards away from the aircraft. We sat down [!] and, after about half a minute, I saw that both engines were burning at the cylinder heads. I went back and climbed into the cockpit, switching off all the switches and looked for the fire extinguisher. I was unable to find it so gathered handfuls of soil and threw them on to the engines [!]. As most of the top of the starboard engine cowling had been burnt away, I was able to put soil right on the fire in that engine; this seemed to be effective and the flames went out. We walked to the nearest road and were picked up by the ambulance. On examination of the aircraft later, it was discovered that the engine trouble was caused by both glycol[12] tanks being holed by debris from the e/a.

Later, when filling in his logbook, he summarises thus:

SCRAMBLE. – 3 JU 188S DESTROYED. A/C HIT BY DEBRIS FROM EXPLODING E/A & ALL GLYCOL LOST. UNABLE TO MAINTAIN HEIGHT FROM 40 MILES OUT & 14000FT. STARBOARD ENGINE CAUGHT FIRE & PORT SEIZED WHEN IN FUNNELS – PRANGED 250 YDS SHORT OF FLARE PATH. .50 [MINS].

Before looking at the ramifications of this incident for Joe and Geoff, it is worth taking a moment to find out the context, and what else happened.

All told, 25 Squadron launched eleven Mosquitos that night, but only the first two made contact with the enemy bomber force. Douggie Greaves and Charlie Robbins, who took off immediately behind Joe and Geoff at the scramble, were directed on to the bombers in the stream that got past Joe and Geoff. They intercepted and destroyed a Do 217 at 2128 hrs, almost exactly the same time as Joe bagged his second 188. And, as Joe was limping home, at 2148 hrs, they shot down a Heinkel 177.[13] Both these engagements took place in an area about 30 miles north of Cromer. So that rounded off a successful night for 25 Squadron, with five enemy aircraft added to their tally.

But 25 were not the only squadron providing Mosquito cover that night. 307 (Polish) Squadron, from Coleby Grange south of Lincoln, had a Mosquito on patrol when the German raid was spotted inbound.

It was crewed by Pilot Officer Prochocki (Pilot) and Flight Lieutenant Zilnkowski (Nav/Rad); they were directed to intercept. There were no times attributed to their engagement but, judging by their report, when they shot down an He177, 12 miles east-north-east of Skegness, they were in amongst the bombers at about the same time as Greaves and Robbins. In addition, 264 (Madras Presidency) Squadron was, despite still being at Church Fenton a long way north, once again fighting alongside 25 Squadron. Their ORB relates that, having scrambled two Mosquitos at around 2120 hrs:

> ...*hostiles began to appear in the Humber and off the North Norfolk coast. Bombs reported at Mablethorpe, Hull, Grimsby and scattered country districts in Lincoln[shire]. F/O R. L. J. Barbour (Pilot) and F/O G Paine (Nav/Rad) obtained a fortuitous contact and saw a Do 217...*

This they duly shot down: their claim is corroborated by the Observer Corps who reported an enemy aircraft crashing five miles north-east of Horncastle at 2208 hrs; so they were mopping up behind the others. In another quirky coincidence, after their combat, Barbour and Paine, suffered an engine failure due to overheating and were obliged to carry out a 'belly landing' at Church Fenton, when they were unable to get their undercarriage down. They landed at 2313 hrs and both were unhurt. So, just in that sector, seven German aircraft were shot down for the loss of two Mosquitos.

Returning to Joe and Geoff's exploits, reliable subsequent research by Chris Goss and others, points to the target of the Luftwaffe's raid that night being Hull. Joe and Geoff, who were first on the scene and attacked the leading aircraft, were not to know it, but they appear to have taken out the German's pathfinder[14] leader – a Hauptmann Walter Schmitt and his crew of four. Which of his three kills was Schmitt is not known but, the fact that he took out three, including Schmitt, and therefore the kernel of the pathfinders, almost certainly threw the entire raid into confusion, and certainly off their objective – hardly any bombs dropped on the target. Of course, it is pure conjecture but Joe and Geoff may well have saved many lives on the ground in Hull that night. In 1991, Joe was asked by 25 Squadron to comment on what he could remember of that night for the Squadron History. His full response is in the Appendix and after extensive research of his own Joe wrote this, regarding the intended target of his victims:

> *The target was Hull. The three Pathfinders were spearheading the raid and were all sowing DUPEL (Window/Chaff) in large quantities. Geoff Haslam did a brilliant job in working through it. With the loss of the pathfinders, the raid was a failure as reported by the Yorkshire Evening News (I believe on the 20th) that: '...although the size of the raid was comparable to those recently attacking London, only 75% of the force managed to cross the coast ... none reached their intended objective and only sporadic bombing developed.'*

The records indicate that Joe and Geoff received only slight wounds in the crash landing, which happened a little before 2200 hrs. The ambulance that picked them up, since they were only just short of the runway threshold, came from RAF Coltishall's own rescue crews. Joe and Geoff would have been taken to the Station Medical Centre for a check-up, released to give their post-Combat Report to the Squadron Intelligence Officer (Flight Lieutenant F. Burchell) and then would be looking forward to post-victory celebrations, with the other crews on stand-by. The events they have just been through have much wider significance than they probably realise at this stage. But somebody else has; the publicity machine has already been set in train; photographers are waiting. In later years, Joe annotates a photograph[15] of himself and Geoff, surrounded by colleagues apparently listening to their story, as taken in Coltishall Mess about 0100 hrs on 20th March. So this widely circulated shot, of them shortly after their traumatic evening, is authentic enough, even if the scene has a distinct staged-for-camera look about it: Joe's head dressing looks fairly convincing, but Geoff looks distinctly ill-at-ease in his knotted handkerchief and the cove next but one to Joe's left, looks as if he would rather get back to the bar.

This photo represents a defining moment in Joe and Geoff's careers – they are about to become national figures – as Joe says, it is destined to be used the same day by the national press. In fact, the *Lancashire Daily Post* is the first to run the story (though without this particular

4 *The Lancashire Daily Post, Monday, March 20, 1944.*

Leyland Pilot Downs 3 Huns, Crash-lands, Puts Out Fire

Flt.-Lieut. J. Singleton

F/LT. JOSEPH SINGLETON, D.F.C., of Leyland, and his observer, F/O. W. J. Haslam, fought four successful battles last night—three against the enemy in the air and one against fire on the ground.

They shot down three raiders in succession as they approached eastern England, and when nearing their base after their victory both engines of their aircraft cut out.

Ground staff at the station heard they had crash - landed in a ploughed field, but after a few minutes of suspense came news of their safety.

Both had climbed out of their aircraft, unhurt, and put the fire out themselves.

Three JU188s

"The three enemy aircraft we destroyed were all JU188s," said F/Lt. Singleton. "The first exploded, and bits of the debris hit our aircraft as the Hun dived steeply and disintegrated.

"The second blew up when hit, and the third, after its starboard engine had caught fire, went down to another burst of firing. We could see blazing bits flying off the plane.

"On the way back to base we had engine trouble when we were down to 200 feet. The starboard engine caught alight, and the other cut when I tried to get everything possible out of it to make base.

Force Landing

" When we force landed, I found both engines were burning. Gently we threw soil over the engine and put the fires out."

Twice in the last month Singleton and Haslam have shot down enemy raiders attacking Britain.

Their first victim was a Dornier 217, which was sent in flames into the sea, and the second, last Tuesday night, was a Ju.188, which broke into two before hitting the ground.

Both are former instructors and were business men before the war.

Flight Lieut. Singleton joined the R.A.F.V.R. as an A/C2 in September, 1939, and later spent eight months teaching new pilots the tricks of operational flying.

Haslam, who comes from West London, was for 18 months instructing night-fighter observers.

A WAR
or Japs | **They walked home from a sky-battle**

DAILY EXPRESS

Daily Express
March 1st 1944.

BREAKFAST after the battle in the squadron mess yesterday. In the centre, with bandaged head, is Flight-Lieut. Joseph Singleton, D.F.C., night-fighter pilot; the other bandage belongs to the navigator, Flying Officer W. J. Haslam. They have just destroyed three Ju.188s in 20 minutes.

As their fighter was coming home to base the starboard engine went on fire, the port engine cut. They force-landed, put out the fire with earth—and walked two miles back to base in the dark.

Above: Lancashire Daily Post; *left:* Daily Express; *both 20th March 1944.*

photo) in their late edition on Monday the 20th. As can be seen from the press cuttings, the *Post* has closely followed Joe through all his exploits and has a good record of getting the facts right. The nationals carry the story (with the photo) on Tuesday morning, with the usual embellishments of the facts – the *Express* reports that, after crashing and putting the aircraft fire out, they '…walked two miles back to base in the dark.' The press coverage is, however, just the start.

ANALYSIS

Geoff Coughlin: Junkers Ju 188 or Junkers Ju 88?

It's clear when looking at all the available evidence that Joe and Geoff shot down three Luftwaffe enemy aircraft on the night of 19th/20th March 1944 and the purpose of this section is to try to bring a little clarity to this subject. It may not matter to some who read these words, indeed Joe and Geoff I'm sure will have been pleased to have simply stopped another three German raiders reaching their target – Hull, but for completeness sake and in the interests of providing a balanced and accurate record of Joe's operational career we have included the following information.

A primary source for what you are about to read comes from what many consider to be the definitive record of 'Operation *Steinbock*'[16] and the information there makes very interesting reading and I recommend this book wholeheartedly for the author's attention to detail, thoroughness and readability. In addition, research by renowned historian Chris Goss also offers insights and evidence referred to above.

To most people, the 'Blitz' lasted from September 1940 to May 1941. However, in December 1943, the code-breakers at Bletchley Park received intelligence that the Luftwaffe's bombers were gathering for a major new operation. The Luftwaffe named the campaign Operation *Steinbock* and committed 524 bombers, including 46 He177 'Greif' four-engined heavy bombers making their debut over Britain.

On the evening of 21st January 1944, 227 bombers took off bound for London, their target marked by Pathfinders from KG66. On their

Junkers Ju 188. German Federal Archives.

Junkers Ju 88 – very similar in size and shape to the Junkers Ju 188 developed from it. German Federal Archives.

return to base, those bombers still serviceable were refuelled and rearmed and in the early morning 220 aircraft repeated the attack. For the next four months, attacks continued against London, Hull, Bristol and other targets in what was the Luftwaffe's final attempt to bomb Britain in strength. Civilian casualties totalled 1,556 killed, with 2,916 seriously injured. The Luftwaffe lost 330 aircraft and their crews – for every five people killed on the ground, the raiders lost one bomber and four trained crewmen killed or captured.

On 19th/20th March, the night when Joe and Geoff claimed their three German raiders in thirteen minutes the focus of *'Steinbock'* operations had switched to the northern city of Hull a major commercial port on England's eastern seaboard. What happened next for Joe and Geoff is fully detailed above and it is clear from their observations on the night, combat records and subsequent recollections that they believed they shot down three Junkers Ju 188s on this sortie. This is completely understandable given the similarity in shape, outline and size of both aircraft, indeed, a casual look at the above photographs shows how similar these aircraft were. Both twin-engined medium

Junkers Ju 88 C6 F8+BX. © Simon Schatz.

bombers most likely similarly marked in general terms with the Junkers Ju188 featuring a slightly more bulbous 'greenhouse' canopy glazing, more pointed wing tips and squarer fin. Apart from that they look very similar.

German losses 19th/20th March 1944

Mackay has reported on German losses before 'Last Blitz' in the seminal work The Blitz – Then and Now although space precluded more detailed information being added at that time. The paucity of information available has also been a factor and interestingly, German records for Luftwaffe losses (LQMG) for the entire year of 1944 have not survived and had to be pieced together from other sources. Fortunately, in recent years the RAF's Air Intelligence department A12(k) (plus interrogation of Luftwaffe aircrew) has been released and freely available in the National Archives. Added to that the continuing work by several researchers and we can begin to draw some vital data and reasonable conclusions about the three aircraft actually shot down on the night of 19th/20th March 1944 by Joe and Geoff.

Key

Hauptmann (Hptm.)	=	Flight Lieutenant
Oberfeldwebel (Ofw.)	=	Flight Sergeant
Feldwebel (Fw.)	=	Sergeant
Unteroffizier (Uffz.)	=	Corporal
Obergefreiter (Ogefr.)	=	Leading Aircraftsman
Gefreiter (Gefr.)	=	Aircraftman First Class
F	=	Flugzeugführer (Pilot)
B	=	Beobachter (Observer – Navigator/Bomb Aimer)
Bf	=	Bordfunker (Wireless (W/T) Operator)
Bs	=	Bordschütze (Gunner)
Bm	=	Bordmechaniker (Flight Mechanic)

Specific aircraft and crews

Do217M 2/KG2 U5+RL WNr 56055

Vicarage Fields, Leybourne, nr Louth, Lincs 2204 hrs

Shot down by F/O R.L.J. Barbour in a 264 Sqn Mosquito.

Uffz Jakob (F), Gefreiter Meinel (B) was the sole survivor among the four-man crew.

Do217M-1 7/KG2 (a/c from 8/KG2 crew from 7/KG2) U5+FS WNr 6262

Failed to return from sortie to Hull

Uffz Johann Glombitza (F) (missing), Uffz Herbert Kallabis (B) (missing), Uffz Heinz Oehme (Bf) (missing), Uffz Heinz Vetters (Bs) (missing).

Ju88 5/KG30 4D+NN WNr 550742

Failed to return from sortie to Hull

Ofw Werner Weil (F) (missing), Ogefr Gerd Schipke (B) (missing), Fw Konrad Meyer (Bf) (missing), Fw Ludwig Leibig (Bs) (missing).

Ju88 5/KG30 4D+GN WNr 883970

Failed to return from sortie to Hull

Fw Fritz Stenutz (F) (missing), Ogefr Albert Vogt (B) (missing), Uffz Walter Schmidt (Bf) (killed), Uffz Willi Mühlendhaupt (Bs) (missing). The body of Walter Schmidt was recovered from the sea.

Ju88 5/KG30 4D+LN WNr 800966

Failed to return from sortie to Hull

Uffz Ulrich Gerlach (F) (missing), Ogefr Gerhard Zobler (B) (missing), Ogefr Karl-Heinz Fischer (Bf) (missing), Gefr Gunther Baus (Bs) (missing).

Ju88 1/KG54 B3+CH WNr 014293

Failed to return from sortie to Hull

Lt Ferdinand Stadtmüller (F) (missing), Uffz Willi Boderke (B) (missing), Uffz Rudolf Heman (Bf) (missing), Uffz Walter Plate (Bs) (missing).

Ju88 6/KG30 4D+AP WNr 550143

Failed to return from sortie to Hull

Fw Rudolf Junger (F) (missing), Ogefr Helmut Westerworth (B) (missing), Ogefr Alfred Müller (Bf) (missing), Gefr Helmut Barth (Bs) (missing).

Ju188E-12/KG66 Z6+EK WNr 260310

Believed to be the aircraft claimed shot down by Humber AA guns at 8,000 ft and crashed in the sea five miles north of the Humber Light Ship. Crash witnessed by several local trawler crews.

Hptmn Walter Schmitt Stkp (F) (missing), Lt Josef Antwerpen (B) (missing), Uffz Wolfgang Krum (Bf) (missing), Uffz Günter Struve (B) (missing), Fw Otto Samus (Bf) (missing).

He177 A-32/KG100 6N+OK WNr 2375

Shot down by P/O J Brochocki in a Mosquito from 307 Sqn and crashed in sea off Skegness during operations to Hull. The claim was confirmed by an ROC post situated at Skegness. 2146 hrs.

Hptm Heinrich Müller (F) (missing), Ogefr Fritz Küchler (Bo) (missing), Uffz Ernst Gundner (Bf) (missing), Uffz Eberhard Hockauf (Bm) (missing), Heinrich Rodenstein (Bs) (missing), Ogefr Werner Utikal (Bs) (missing).

It seems likely, therefore, that Joe and Geoff in fact shot down Junkers Ju188E-12/KG66 Z6+EK WNr 260310 (although claimed by Humber AA guns – see above). In addition, it also seems probable that Joe and Geoff also shot down two Junkers Ju88 aircraft from those listed above.

Inevitably, trying to accurately attribute specific German aircraft losses to Joe and Geoff is an inexact science, but it is hoped that this brief analysis of the available information may shed a little more light on what actually happened.

11.

Aftermath

(21st March–23rd June 1944)

When they reappear at 25 Squadron Dispersal after some rest on the Monday, the messages start coming in. A signal is received from the Air Officer Commanding 12 Group – Air Vice-Marshal M. Henderson – congratulating the whole Squadron for the previous night's fine effort and 'ESPECIALLY MAGNIFICENT SHOW' put up by Joe, Geoff, Greaves and Robbins. Another signal from Chief of the Air Staff, Charles Portal, is along similar lines but singles out Joe and Geoff's achievement for his personal admiration which he describes as:

> ... A BRILLIANT FEAT OF ARMS AND THEIR SAFE LANDING WITH BOTH ENGINES ON FIRE WAS A SPLENDID PIECE OF AIRMANSHIP.

Such was the impact of the 'Three-in-Thirteen' that the Commander-in-Chief of Fighter Command – Air Marshal Sir Roderic Hill flew in to Coltishall to discuss the events of the previous night, and personally congratulate Joe and Geoff. Joe later recorded:

```
From:-  Headquarters, No. 12 Group

To  :-  No. 25 Squadron.

A.350.  20 MAR.   A.O.C. SENDS HEARTIEST CONGRATULATIONS ON SQUADRON'S FINE
                  EFFORT LAST NIGHT. ESPECIALLY MAGNIFICENT SHOW PUT UP BY
                  SINGLETON HASLAM GREAVES AND ROBBINS. HOPE YOU WILL SOON
                  GET FURTHER SUCCESSFUL HUNTING.


From:-  Air Ministry, Whitehall.

To  :-  W/C. Wight-Boycott. DSO.

A.320   20 MAR.   WARMEST CONGRATULATIONS TO YOU AND ALL RANKS OF 25 SQUADRON
                  ON THE DESTRUCTION OF 5 ENEMY AIRCRAFT LAST NIGHT. PLEASE
                  CONVEY TO FLIGHT LIEUTENANT SINGLETON AND FLYING OFFICER
                  HASLAM MY PERSONAL ADMIRATION FOR THEIR OUTSTANDING ACHIEVEMENT
                  IN SHOOTING DOWN THREE OF THESE ENEMY AIRCRAFT IN A SINGLE
                  SORTIE TWO OF THEM AFTER ONE ENGINE HAD STOPPED. IT WAS A
                  BRILLIANT FEAT OF ARMS AND THEIR SAFE LANDING WITH BOTH
                  ENGINES ON FIRE WAS A SPLENDID PIECE OF AIRMANSHIP.


From:-  10 Group

To  :-  No. 25 Squadron.

P.722   17 APR.   FOLLOWING MESSAGES RECEIVED. FIRST MESSAGE FROM A.E.A.F BEGINS
                  HIS MAJESTY THE KING ON THE RECOMMENDATION OF THE AIR COMMANDER
                  IN CHIEF HAS BEEN GRACIOUSLY PLEASED TO AWARD THE DISTINGUISHED
                  SERVICE ORDER TO F/LT. J.SINGLETON NO. 25 SQUADRON.
                  SECOND MESSAGE FROM A.D.G.B. BEGINS AIR MARSHAL COMMANDING
                  AIR DEFENCE OF GREAT BRITAIN SENDS HIS WARMEST CONGRATULATIONS
                  TO F/LT. J.SINGLETON ON HIS AWARD OF THE DISTINGUISHED SERVICE
                  ORDER.
                  A.O.C. 10 GROUP EXTENDS HEARTIEST CONGRATULATIONS.
```

Congratulatory signals. Singleton Private Collection.

This was a very private visit known only to a few on the station. Apart from his immediate interest in the combats, he also wanted to know [any advice we could provide on] how other Nav. Rads. could work through similar window [Luftwaffe Dupel] conditions etc.

RAF Coltishall's ORB describes Hill as 'C-in-C A.D.G.B.' (Air Defence of Great Britain). This is less confusing than it might appear. At this time, the whole of Britain's Armed Forces were beginning to get geared up for the invasion of France. In anticipation of this, Fighter Command had ostensibly split into the Second Tactical Air Force – those squadrons earmarked to support the Invasion, and the ADGB – those earmarked to maintain the air defence of the

British Homeland. At this stage, several months before the Invasion, the ADGB was indistinguishable from Fighter Command as it had been since the war began. But the new titles were already appearing within the RAF's organisations. The BBC's Stewart Macpherson may be remembered as the Canadian broadcaster whose calm but tense commentary, on location in the back of an RAF Lancaster as it carried out a bombing run over Germany, graphically depicted the terrors and destruction of a Bomber Command crew's world. Late on the Monday evening (20th March), Joe relates that he and Geoff recorded an interview with Stewart Macpherson, which was broadcast on the mid-day overseas BBC News the next day (21st March). This was undoubtedly for propaganda purposes, as well as home consumption. Stewart Macpherson went on to beat Winston Churchill into second place for the *Daily Mail's* Voice of the Year Competition in 1946. He was the first chairman of BBC Radio's *Twenty Questions.*

Rather more cryptic was this telegram, from 'Wilson and Davies', suggesting Geoff enjoyed spinning lines:

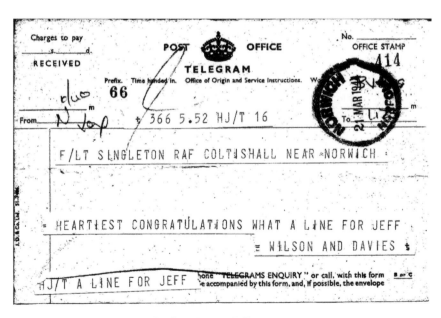

Singleton Private Collection.

On 24th March, Marshal of the RAF Lord Portal follows up his signal of the 20th with a personal letter to Joe.

AIR MINISTRY.
KING CHARLES STREET
WHITEHALL S.W.I.

24th March 1944.

My dear Singleton,

I have read with the greatest interest the account of your exploit last Sunday night, when you brought down three JU.188s and then managed to do a successful belly-landing after one engine had caught fire. It reflects the greatest credit on yourself and your navigator and I am delighted that you managed to escape safely. My heartiest congratulations to you both.

Yours sincerely

C. Portal.

Flight Lieutenant J.A. Singleton, D.F.C.,
R.A.F. Station, Coltishall,
Norwich,
Norfolk.

Flight Lieutenant J.A. Singleton, D.F.C.,
R.A.F. Station, Coltishall,
Norwich,
Norfolk.

CHIEF OF THE AIR STAFF.

Letter CAS Lord Portal. Singleton Private Collection.

At some stage during the aftermath of the now famous night, Joe would have been told that his actions were to be rewarded with an 'Immediate' Distinguished Service Order (DSO). 'Immediate' refers to the award being for a specific act of gallantry rather than a cumulative period of gallant conduct as, for instance, his DFC had been. Normally, an award recommendation is initially written up by the subject's commanding officer. It is then sent up the chain of command through the various levels until it reaches the Commander-in-Chief who will decide if the case merits an award from his limited quota. All this takes considerable time for the wheels to turn and it could be months from recommendation to award. However, if a gallant deed is brought to the attention of a sufficiently senior officer (in this case probably Charles Portal) who considers it warrants an award, a discussion takes place with the appropriate member of the Royal Household. Portal will put the case and his recommendation for the level of the award, and the Palace representative will be authorised to agree (or not) on behalf of the King. If agreement is reached, the award becomes 'Immediate' by virtue of this much quicker process.

In Joe's case it was approved and no doubt he would have told friends and family first, but the first written sign that it has been made public comes from a rather odd source – in the form of a telegram from the Commanding Officer and men of 25 Squadron to Joe on 17th April, when he was apparently with the Handling Section Rolls Royce in Derby. Maybe Joe had been giving them some feedback on the performance of their Merlins with no glycol for cooling?

A personal letter soon follows these from Commander-in-Chief Roderic Hill via Frank Stannard, a friend of Joe, who was Hill's Personal Staff Officer at Kestrel Grove.[1] That aside, the local and national papers are once again abuzz with the news of Joe's DSO and retelling the three-in-thirteen story.

Joe and Geoff do not fly again until 15th April and his first patrol on the 23rd is eventful, providing more feedback for Rolls Royce.

PATROL – CHASED BOGEY. – STBD ENGINE
CAUGHT FIRE – RETURNED TO BASE.

Top: Distinguished Service Order Signal from 25 Squadron; above left: Letter C-in-C AM Hill; above right: DSO Newspaper Clipping. Singleton Private Collection.

Award promulgated in London Gazette dated 28 April 1944

DISTINGUISHED SERVICE ORDER

Flight Lieutenant Joseph SINGLETON, DFC (69431), Royal
Air Force Volunteer Reserve, No 25 Squadron.

Since being awarded the Distinguished Flying Cross this
officer has completed very many sorties. Within a short
period he has destroyed 5 enemy aircraft at night; 3 of
which he shot down in one sortie. On this occasion his
aircraft was damaged but he flew it to this country.
When nearing an airfield both engines failed and caught
fire. Nevertheless, Flight Lieutenant Singleton effected
a successful crash-landing. After getting clear, Flight
Lieutenant Singleton returned to the burning aircraft and
switched off all the electrical circuits. Afterwards,
unaided, he succeeded in extinguishing the flames by
smothering them with earth. This officer, who displayed
a high degree of courage, coolness and devotion to duty,
undoubtedly saved his aircraft from becoming a total loss.

London
Gazette:
DSO citation.
Singleton
Private
Collection.

The remainder of the month is uneventful for Joe and the *London Gazette* finally catches up with events by promulgating his DSO citation on 28th April 1944.

With the Baby Blitz over, the first two weeks in May were equally quiet and at some stage Joe and Geoff would have been told their days on 25 Squadron were numbered. HQ Fighter Command had selected them for special duties representing a completely different, and far more strategic, contribution to the war effort; they were to take a new Mosquito NF Mk 30 to the United States. The Mk X AI that Joe and Geoff had proved to be so effective was, as already mentioned, in essence, an American Radar, the SCR 720, conceived by MIT scientists and produced by Western Electric. The radars that arrived in the UK were designed specifically for the Northrop P61 Black Widow, and vice

De Havilland Mosquito NF.30 (RK952/MB-24) Photo courtesy Koninklijk Leger Museum, Brussels

versa. Therefore, considerable time and money had to be spent by RAF maintenance units to modify each radar set, for fitting to the Mosquito as the Mk X. Joe and Geoff's main objective was to obtain agreement for those modifications to be made during manufacture, thereby making considerable savings. In addition, they were to share their knowledge and experience with the US fighter communities, in order to find mutually beneficial strategies for taking night fighting into the future.

Joe and Geoff say their farewells to 25 Squadron on 17th May and, with over 1,400 hours of flying, over 250 of which are on multi-engines at night, the Commanding Officer Wing Commander Wight-Boycott, signs Joe off in his logbook as an 'Exceptional' night fighter pilot.

Finally getting the recognition he so richly deserves, Geoff Haslam is gazetted for the DFC on 26th May 1943. Naturally, it had gone through the long not the 'Immediate' channels but, no doubt, it was celebrated just as heartily, especially by Joe.

Having made their way to HQ ADGB at Stanmore, they receive their top secret briefings and wait for their new aircraft to be made ready.

Flt Lt Joe Singleton DSO DFC and Fg Off Geoff Haslam DFC. Singleton Private Collection.

They also have to learn a whole new branch of aviation – trans-Atlantic navigation. But they have one last 'hurrah' up their sleeves. Borrowing a Mosquito (MM415) from 605 Squadron, then based at RAF Manston in Kent, and joining eight 605 Squadron crews on Diver Patrols (specific anti V1 sorties) that night, on 23rd June, Joe records:

> **'DIVER' PATROL – ½ SEC BURST. 1 PILOTLESS A/C DESTROYED OVER CHANNEL. 2.10 [HRS].**

That brought Joe's total to seven aircraft and one V1 'Buzz Bomb' destroyed, three aircraft damaged in the air and one on the ground. They did not know then that they had flown their last combat mission. But there were to be many more, very different, sorts of adventures to come.

Appendix

Contents

Combat Reports of 'Destroyed'

1. 3rd September 1942 – 1 x He 111

COPY.

FORM "F"

FINAL INTELLIGENCE

COMBAT REPORT

Sector Serial No............................ (A).....................AI/81

Serial No of Order detailing Flight or
Squadron to Patrol......................... (B)................................

Date... (C)..............3/9/42...........

Flight, Squadron............................ (D) Flight:....A....Sqdn...25.....

Number of Enemy Aircraft.................... (E)..............One...............

Type of Enemy Aircraft...................... (F)..............HE.111...........

Time Attack was Delivered................... (G)............2250 hours.........

Place Attack was delivered.................. (H)....20 miles E. of FILEY......

Height of Enemy............................. (J).........16-17,000 feet........

Enemy Casualties............................ (K)......1 HE.111 Destroyed......

Our Casualties.....Nil.......Aircraft....Nil... (L)..........Nil.............

Personnel....Nil... (M)..........Nil.............

SEARCHLIGHTS - Was enemy illuminated, if not,   N/A
were they in front or behind the target.   (N i)......................

A.A. GUNS - Did shell burst assist pilot in   N/A
intercepting the enemy.   (N ii).....................

GENERAL REPORT

One Beaufighter I Mark IV A.I. 25 Squadron, Rajah 20, Pilot Fg.Off Singleton, Operator Plt Off Bradshaw, took off Church Fenton 2150 hours, landed Base 2357 hours. Taken over by Easington C.H.L. 2205 hours, put on patrol line 75 miles off Flamborough flying at 12,000 feet. When on this patrol control informed pilot that bandit was coming in from the East and to increase height to 14,000 feet. Contact was obtained on E/A on course 260 degrees at maximum range flying at 17,000 feet. E/A being 3,000 feet above fighter, to starboard. Fighter climbed to 17,500 feet visual obtained on exhausts of E/A at 3,500 feet range. E/A still being slightly above fighter. The speed of E/A 140 m.p.h. A.S.I., which was taking only very gentle evasive action dips and climbs of 1,000 feet, but maintaining average height 17,500 feet. Visual maintained and from exhausts E/A appeared to be HE.111. Fighter continued chase did not carry out attack although no resins or I.F.F. showing until further identification was possible. Fighter continued to stalk E/A maintaining A.I. contact and visual following at 400 yards slightly below and dead astern, until at 2250 hours 20 miles from coast E. of Filey, closed to 100-125 yards range and was able to identify E/A as HE.111 from silhouette and exhausts. Fighter opened fire from 100 yards range giving a 1½-2 seconds burst, which was immediately followed by a large white flash and explosion. Further short burst fired into area of flash, the E/A then disappeared from pilot's view going down, but was seen by operator to be going down on fire. Pilot regained sight of E/A after a

Signature

O.C.   (Section
       (Flight
       (Squadron   Squadron No.

-2-

short time and E/A was then seen burning on the sea. Pilot's opinion is that strikes from the first attack hit bombs which exploded.

Observer Corps reported seeing fire at sea in position and time of combat.

Easington C.H.L. Controller was very efficient and assisted greatly in the destruction of this E/A. Controller - Flt Lt Trollope

Weather - 5/10 cloud 10,000 feet clear sky above. Visibility above clouds variable.

Ammunition expended - 20 mm.   203
                          303   497

Our Casualties   Nil.   Enemy Casualties   1 HE.111 Destroyed.

(Signed) :-   D. McReady   Fg Off

Intelligence Officer
No   25   Squadron.

2. 17th/18th May 1943 – Op Ranger: 3 Trains.

COPY   FORM "F"

INTELLIGENCE COMBAT REPORT

Date	(A)	Night 17th/18th May 1943
Unit	(B)	No 25 Squadron.
Type and Mark of Our Aircraft	(C)	Mosquito IIF.
Time Attack was Delivered	(D)	Trains attacked between 0040 and 0050 hours.
Place of Attack and/or Target	(E)	(1) Loco. 4 miles E. of LUBBECKE
		(2) 2 Locos. south of HILLE.
Weather	(F)	Good - Visibility Excellent.
Our Casualties - Aircraft	(G)	Nil
Our Casualties - Personnel	(H)	Nil
Enemy Casualties in Combat	(J)	Nil
Enemy Casualties - Ground or Sea	(K)	One loco. seriously damaged and two locomotives damaged.

GENERAL REPORT

One Mosquito IIF, No 25 Squadron, Pilot Flt Lt SINGLETON, Navigator Sgt SKINNER took off from COLTISHALL at 2300 hours 17/5/43 to attack transportation targets on Ranger Route No 8. Crossed Dutch Coast North of VLIELAND at 2340 hours at 4,000 feet. Set course for HARLINGEN, ASSEN, thence for a point S.W. of OLDENBURG and on E.T.A. struck KUSTEN CANEL. Course was then set for SYKE, and, approximately 16 miles S.E. of OLDENBURG objects later identified as two factory chimneys, situated alongside a railway line emitting white smoke, closely resembling a moving train, were fired at in the mistaken belief that they were locomotives. Two bursts of Cannon and M/G each of 1 - 2 seconds duration were given from 200 feet. Strikes were observed. Continued patrol and sighted a railway line running into SULINGEN which was orbitted at 2,000 feet at 0030 hours in an unsuccessful search for suitable targets, so the centre of the town was then ground straffed with a 4 - 5 seconds burst with Cannon and M/G from about 100 feet. The railway line leading south from SULINGEN was then patrolled in a search for a target and a slow moving westbound train was sighted and attacked approximately 4 miles east of LUBBECKE. A burst with Cannon and M/G of 2 - 3 seconds duration from abeam was given and numerous strikes were observed on the locomotive which emitted clouds of steam and the train stopped. Whilst turning to starboard with the intention of carrying out a further attack a second train, travelling in a southerly direction was sighted south of HILLE, and this was attacked from abeam with a 2 - 3 seconds burst with Cannon and M/G. Strikes were observed on the locomotive which emitted clouds of steam and the train became stationary. Whilst pulling out to starboard a third train, northward bound, again south of HILLE was seen upon which a beam attack was made with a 2 - 3 seconds burst of Cannon and M/G. Strikes were seen on the engine and the train came to a standstill. A further attack from the port quarter was carried out on the last mentioned train with a burst of 2 - 3 secons duration with Cannon and M/G. Strikes were seen again on the engine which emitted clouds of sparks into the air up to a height of 100 feet, and great

quantities of steam. Following upon this, the second train, which
was still stationary was given a burst of 2 - 3 seconds from abeam
with both Cannon and M/G. Strikes were again seen on the loco.
from which still more smoke poured. A further attack was then made
on the first train with a 2 - 3 seconds burst from Cannon and M/G.
and strikes were seen on the still stationary loco. This was
followed by a further burst from both Cannon and M/G. on the first
train of approximately 1 second duration but no strikes were seen
on this occasion. Mosquito then set course for Base pinpointing
EDAM at 3,000 feet at 0124 hours and re-crossing the Dutch coast at
0128 hours 5 miles north of IJMUIDEN at 3,500 feet landing at CHURCH
FENTON at 0235 hours. On the inward journey a double-yellow flare
fired from the ground was observed S.W. of OLDENBURG and a similar
one was seen at RHEINE on the return journey.

The patrol was carried out at heights between 2,000 and 2,500 feet.

Pilot	No of Rounds fired & ammo. used.	Length of Burst, Range and direction of attack.	Cine Camera Gun
Flt Lt SINGLETON	20 M.M. Cannon. A.P. 386 rounds HE/INC. 388 rounds .303 Brownings A.P. 293 rounds Mk.VI Inc. 293 rounds	With the exception of the 4th attack on the locomotives (which was carried out with a 2 - 3 seconds burst from the port quarter, opening at 600 feet closing to 150 feet the remainder of attacks on locos. were from abeam opening at 1,000 feet closing to 300 feet with bursts of 2 - 3 seconds each.	EXPOSED

(Signed) :-   E.K. DAVIES   Fg Off

Intelligence Officer
No 25 Squadron, R.A.F.
CHURCH FENTON.

3. 17th/18th May 1943 – Op Ranger: 3 Trains.

COPY   FORM "F"

COMBINED INTELLIGENCE AND PERSONAL
COMBAT REPORT

Date.   (A). 11th June 1943

Unit.   (B). No 25 Squadron detached to
                                                    No 264 Squadron PREDANNACK.

Type and Mark of our Aircraft.   (C). Mosquito IIF.

Time Attack was Delivered.   (D). 1620 hours.

Place of Attack and/or Target.   (E). JU.88 at Position 45° 25'N.
                                                                       7° 45'W.

Weather.   (F). 5/10ths Cloud at 2000 feet
                                                    Visibility 15 miles.

Our Casualties - Aircraft.   (G). NIL

   "   "   - Personnel.   (H). NIL

Enemy Casualties in Combat.   (J). One JU.88 DESTROYED.

   "   "   Ground or Sea.   (K). NIL

GENERAL REPORT

        Mosquito IIF No 25 Squadron (detached to No 264 Squadron)
Pilot Flt Lt J. SINGLETON, Navigator Fg Off W.G. HASLAM (BLUE1) took
off from PREDANNACK at 1430 hours 11th June on INSTEP patrol No 147
leading a formation of six aircraft consisting of BLUE and GREEN
sections, GREEN section being led by Flt Lt PANITZ (GREEN 1).

        Formation flew in two VICS in loose line astern lead by
BLUE 1. At 1459 hours a course of 218 degrees was set and at 1505
hours GREEN 1 reported engine trouble and returned to base, and
GREEN 2 and GREEN 3 (Fg Off NEWELL and Flt Sgt RICHARDSON respectively)
thereupon took up positions as BLUE 4 and BLUE 5 respectively. At
approximately 1617 hours BLUE 2 (Fg Off WOOTTON) reported sighting a
formation of five E/A identified as Ju.88's at position 9 o' clock,
and flying in loose Echelon to starboard at a height of 5000 - 6000
feet. The height of the formation was then 50 feet. BLUE 1 ordered
formation to close, and to commence climbing in order to get into
the sun, instructing BLUE 3 and BLUE 5 to operate as a section and
BLUE 2 and BLUE 4 to remain with the LEADER, the section led by BLUE 1
flew a gap in the cloud at 2000 feet, climbing at the rate of 2000 feet
per minute, keeping the E/A in sight.

        Section was then obviously seen by the E/A because they
altered course and commenced a climbing orbit to port in loose line
astern. Three of the enemy aircraft were successively seen to fire
a three star red cartridge. Section continued to climb to manoeuvre
into the sun with the enemy aircraft down sun, and, at the same time,
the enemy aircraft were attempting to outfly the section to gain the
same advantage. When enemy aircraft were approximately 2000 feet
above the section, BLUE 1 ordered Section, which was then at 5500 feet
to break and go into attack. Shortly afterwards, BLUE 1 experienced

                                          /fire...

fire simultaneously from three or four of the enemy aircraft at a
range of 3000 - 4000 feet. The fire was seen to come from the
dorsal turret in all cases, the tracer passing well above Mosquito.
The bursts from each enemy aircraft were of approximately 2 seconds
duration and M/G only. BLUE 1 selected the rearmost enemy aircraft
in the formation, which was nearest to him, and, doing a climbing
turn to port inside the enemy aircraft at an I.A.S. of approximately
170 m.p.h. opened fire when about 200 feet below enemy aircraft with
a full deflection shot of 70 degrees, giving a short burst of less
than one seconds' duration with cannon only (the M/G's failing to
fire), from approximately 800 yards range. The enemy aircraft's
port engine emitted considerable volumes of thick black smoke, and
the enemy aircraft peeled off to starboard in a dive. BLUE 1
followed on his tail and gave another short burst of approximately
1 second from dead astern and slightly above with cannon only, from
approximately 300 yards range, and sheets of flame were seen outboard
of the enemy aircraft's port engine. Return M/G fire was experienced
from the dorsal position of the enemy aircraft, but Mosquito was not
hit. Enemy aircraft then pulled out of dive, and BLUE 1 followed,
gained on enemy aircraft and closing in to within 25 yards gave
another 3 second burst (cannon only) from dead astern whilst closing
right in and flames inboard of the port engine, followed by black
smoke emitted from the enemy aircraft's starboard were observed.
Mosquito's windscreen thereupon became covered with oil from the
enemy aircraft, which made sighting difficult, and he was compelled
to peel off suddenly to starboard to avoid colliding with enemy
aircraft, which was simultaneously observed to go into a steep dive.
BLUE 1 again turned into the attack, followed and overtook the
enemy aircraft and, from slightly above enemy aircraft at a range
of 500 feet, gave a burst of approximately 1 second from the starboard
quarter, at an angle of 45 degrees. Bits of cowling from the starboard
engine, and pieces of the enemy aircraft's mainplane flew off as a
result of the attack. Immediately afterwards, as BLUE 1 passed above
and behind enemy aircraft, two of the enemy aircraft's crew were seen
to bale out. One was observed to make his exit through the top hatch
and was struck a glancing blow by the port tailplane of the enemy
aircraft, which then turned over and in a vertical dive, entered the
sea. BLUE 1 orbitted at about 2000 feet, and climbed through a gap
in the cloud to search for more "game"; but no enemy aircraft were
seen, so instructed section to return to base. A cine camera exposure
of the oil patch which marked the spot where the enemy aircraft hit
the sea, was taken before returning to base. The combat commenced at
a height of 7500 feet and continued down to approximately 2000 feet.
Formation landed at PREDANNACK between 1800 - 1808 hours.

Enemy Casualties : One JU.88 Destroyed.
Own   "   :   NIL.

Pilot.	No of Rounds fired and type of ammunition used.	Length of Burst Range and Direction of Attack.	Cine Camera Gun
Flt Lt	20 mm. Cannon.	1. Deflection less than one second from 800 yards.	Exposed.
J. SINGLETON	Port Outer 45 rounds " Inner 47 " Stbd Outer 47 " " Inner 44 "	2. Dead Astern 1 second from 300 yards.	
	No stoppages. M/Gs failed to fire owing to electrical defect.	3. Dead Astern 3 seconds from 25 yards.	
		4. Starboard quarter, 1 second from 500 feet.	

(Signed) :-   E.K. DAVIES   Fg Off

Intelligence Officer
No 25   Squadron
R.A.F. CHURCH FENTON.

4. 20th February 1944 – 1 x Do 217

COPY

COMPOSITE REPORT
REF. A.I. 6C9/21 Feb.

R.A.F. STATION, COLTISHALL

FINAL INTELLIGENCE AND PILOT'S PERSONAL COMBAT REPORT FORM "F"
(Ref 25/2/1944).

STATISTICAL.

(A) 20/21 February 1944
(B) 25 Squadron.
(C) Mosquito XVII/A.I. Mk. X.
(D) 2236 hours.
(E) HO513 (50 miles E. of Lowestoft).
(F) 5/10 - 7/10 cloud at 5000 feet. None above : dark, starry.
(G) Nil.
(H) Nil.
(J) 1 Do. 217 Destroyed.
(K) Nil.

GENERAL REPORT

We were scrambled from Coltishall at 2110 hours. Taken over by G.C.I. Neatishead and given vector of 200° and told to climb to Angels 18. On arriving at this height we patrolled on a course of 080 and 200° until handed over at 2143 to C.H.L. Happisburgh (Controller Flt Lt Brodie). We had two chases which turned out to be ineffective due to C.H.L. not being able to help us any further. We were then told that they had a bogey for us going westwards Angels 10. Given vector of 080 and chased for about 15 minutes when at 2228 hours Nav/Rad. obtained contact at 3 miles range, 30° starboard at 9000 feet in position HO333. Target was weaving gently and we closed to 2000 feet. As there was about 5/10-7/10 cloud at 5000 feet it was decided to obtain a visual of bogey silhouetted against the cloud. We closed to about 1000 feet and obtained visual 5 degrees starboard and 5 degrees below. Nav/Rad. used night binoculars and immediately identified e/a as Do. 217 (when flying at 9000 feet 200/230 I.A.S.). Closed in to about 200 yards and pilot also identifying e/a as Do.217 gave a two second burst from dead astern. Strikes were seen on port wing and engine and e/a immediately climbed about 1000 feet, then turning to port with large quantities of sparks pouring from its port engine. We closed in again, it being quite easy to follow the trail of sparks left by e/a and at about 100 yards gave another burst of about 3½ seconds from dead astern scoring strikes on fuselage, port engine and wing root. A big explosion occurred in the port engine and wing root and e/a immediately lost height rapidly, blazing fiercely. We followed him down to about 3000 feet and he suddenly disappeared into the sea in position HO513 (approx.). No return fire was experienced and no exhaust glows were seen from e/a. Went back to C.H.L. and although weapon was behaving badly we obtained contact on a bogey travelling on a vector of 120°. Contact was held for about 15-20 minutes. We came down gently losing height to 6-7000 feet and pulled the boost cut-out (I.A.S. 320/330) but were unable to catch e/a. Petrol was running short and when 20 miles off the Dutch coast contact was lost due to speed of e/a and chase was given up. Returned to base and landed 2340 hours.

Pilot's comment : Excellent controlling by Flt Lt Brodie at Happisburgh.

ARMAMENT REPORT

20 mm. Cannon

H.E.I. 120 rounds.
S.A.P.I. 120 rounds.

OBSERVATIONS.

No. 1 GUN U/S TO 1
GUN. PORT WING U/S.

(Signed) :- J. SINGLETON

    Flt Lt (Pilot).

(Signed) :- D. MELVILLE

    Flying Officer.
    Intelligence Officer
(Signed) :- W.G. Haslam
    Wg Off (Nav/Rad.).
    No 25 Squadron.

5. 14th March 1944 – 1 x Ju 188

<u>COPY</u> COMPOSITE REPORT
R.F. A.I. 832/15 MAR.

FINAL INTELLIGENCE AND PILOT'S PERSONAL COMBAT REPORT FORM "F".

(a) 14/15 March, 1944.
(b) 25 Squadron.
(c) Mosquito XVII.
(d) 2210 hours.
(e) N.0191 (4/6 miles E. of Southwold).
(f) 8/10 Cloud at 4/5000 feet above, dark, starry and clear.
(g) NIL.
(h) Leading edge of starboard mainplane slightly damaged by debris
     from e/a.
(j) 1 JU 188 destroyed.
(k) NIL.

GENERAL REPORT

Took off from Coltishall at 2105 hours and carried out Bullseye
exercise until 22.05 hours, when handed over from Sector Control to
Neatishead G.C.I. and given a vector of 140°. At 18,000 feet asked if
there was any "trade" and told there were "possibilities". A few
minutes later, 22.09 hours, a head on contact was obtained at 4½ miles
10° port and we called up and asked permission to follow it. G.C.I.
gave permission but were unable to help any further towards identificatio
Contact lost in turn but regained as we levelled out. E/a was then
about 16,000 feet height with A.S.I. approximately 240 m.p.h., taking
normal evasive action. We closed in to 1,000 feet and visual obtained
10° to starboard and 10° above, e/a being then in a starboard orbit.
Observer used binoculars and identified a JU188, pilot also identified
and closed in to about 75 yards and gave a three seconds burst from
dead astern. A big explosion occurred in the port side of the fuselage
and the German markings were seen on the underneath side of port wing.
As e/a broke port fighter went to starboard, e/a was then burning
fiercely being astern and to port; as fighter banked port e/a climbed
and went to starboard and then dived steeply and when about 9,000 feet
broke up in two portions each burning fiercely, e/a disappeared into
cloud at 5,000 feet and shortly afterwards explosion and big blaze seen
reflected on cloud. Combat seen by Grampus 22, 27 and 18.

Landed Coltishall 2355 hours. On landing leading edge of
starboard mainplane was found to be slightly damaged by debris.

ARMAMENT REPORT

20 mm. Cannon	Cine Camera
58 rounds S.A.P.I.	Not operated.
58 rounds H.E.I.	

Flt.Lt.Singleton (Pilot)

Fg.Off.Haslam.(Nav/Rad.O.).

(Signed) : F. BURCHELL Flt Lt.

Sector Intelligence Officer,
R.A.F. Station, Coltishall.

6. 19th March 1944 – 3 x Ju 88/188

```
                                        COMPOSITE REPORT
                 COPY.                   REF. A.I. 883/20 MAR.

              R.A.F. STATION, COLTISHALL

        FINAL INTELLIGENCE AND PILOT'S PERSONAL COMBAT REPORT
              FORM "F".  (REF : 25/5/1944).
```

STATISTICAL.

(A) 19/20 March 1944.
(B) 25 Squadron.
(C) Mosquito XVII/AI Mk.X.
(D) (i) 2120 hours. (ii) 2127 hours. (iii) 2133 hours.
(E) (i) H4498 (56 miles NNE Cromer) (ii) C5022 (65 miles NNE Cromer)
     (iii) H5183 (80 miles NNE Cromer).
(F) No cloud ; very dark but starlight.
(G) Flt Lt Singleton, D.F.C. (Pilot) Slight head injuries.
     Pg Off Haslam (Nav/Rad).
(H) Mosquito XVII Cat. E. (Both glycol tanks holed by debris from e/a)
                                      (crash-landed)
(J) 3 Ju188 Destroyed.
(K) Nil.

GENERAL.

We took off from Coltishall at 2055 hours, given a vector of 080°
and handed over from Sector to G.C.I. Neatishead. Told to hurry and climb
to 16,000 ft. When at about 8,000 feet was handed over to C.H.L.
Happisburgh and given vector of 030° and then 010° and told 12 bandits
ahead crossing from starboard to port. When at 16,000 feet contact was
obtained at 8½ miles range, 30° starboard crossing from starboard to
port. We turned to port and followed, closed the range and obtained
visual 10° above at 15,000 feet. Identified as Ju188 (by pilot and
Nav/Rad.) and closed to about 100 yards and gave 2½ sec. burst at 100
yards from dead astern. Strikes were scored on fuselage, immediately
followed by a big explosion. As we were still closing we saw the German
markings on the tail of the Ju188 and had to pull up steeply to avoid
collision; debris from the e/a spattered our aircraft. We orbitted and
watched e/a go down in a steep dive to port in flames. Then the e/a had
dropped about 5,000 feet it broke up completely and several burning
pieces were seen to hit the sea, casting a glow over a wide area. After
fixing the position with G.C.I. Neatishead went back to Happisburgh. Was
given a vector of 190° and whilst turning on to this vector we obtained
a contact at 4½ miles, 15° starboard crossing slowly starboard to port.
With the e/a vectoring about 330° we closed in behind and slightly below
and when at about 1,500 feet range obtained a visual about 10° above
(pilot and Nav/Rad.) both identifying again as a Ju188). Closed in to
about 100 yards range, dead astern. E/a was not taking any evasive
action and a 2½ sec. burst given from dead asten scored strikes and
caused an explosion in the centre of the fuselage. E/a exploded, burst
into flames and went down practically vertically, hit the sea and
continued to burn fiercely on the water. We orbitted and again got a
fix of the position from Neatishead and then went back to Happisburgh.
Almost immediately (no vector given) contact was obtained at 4 miles
range crossing hard starboard to port. We did a hard turn to port and
followed e/a at A.S.I. of 230 and at a height of 16,000 feet. E/a was
taking quite violent evasive action and making rapid alterations of
height. We closed in to about 1,500 feet and obtained visual about 15°
above and slightly to starboard. We identified e/a as a Ju188 and closed
in to 125 yards dead astern, fired a .2½ sec. burst scoring strikes in
starboard engine which emitted large quantities of sparks and the engine
burst into flames. E/a then lost height in a shallow dive. A deflection
shot of 3 secs. duration from 5° above and 5° post at 500 - 600 yards
range scored hits which caused e/a to burst into a mass of flames, bits
of burning debris flying off as it rapidly lost height and hit the sea
where it burned fiercely.

Pilot's narrative of bringing damaged aircraft back to base.

Immediately after combat I found my engines were very rough and
on examination saw that the port Radiator Temperature Gauge was reading
140° and the starboard about 120°. I throttled back, opened radiator

-2-

flaps and got engines a little cooler. I told Happisburgh we were
having engine trouble and was given a vector and told to go over to
G.C.I. Neatishead. The port engine was emitting a lot of sparks and
was very hot so I feathered it. Immediately the starboard engine
overheated so I unfeathered the port and flew with both engines
throttled as far back as practicable without too much loss of height.
(On completion of the third combat we were down to 14,000 feet and
crossed the coast on a vector of 300° at about 5,000 feet.). The
radiator temperatures were each reading 130-140° (so I told Nav/Rad.
to stand by to bale out. I called up base and asked for aerodrome
lighting to be switched on and so could see base from the coast.
Both engines were still running, but very roughly, and we were gently
losing height. I had decided to land with wheels and flaps up) With
an A.S.I. of about 180 I came through the funnels just under 1,000
feet. At this point the starboard engine seized and burst into flames.
I told Nav/Rad. to operate the starboard engine fire extinguisher and
I switched on port landing light since a crash looked inevitable and I
was hoping it would help; unfortunately it was not fully down when we
landed. I tried to get more power out of the port engine which,
however, seized also. We got down into the red of the angle glide then
the red disappeared and with an A.S.I. of 140 I levelled out a bit and
suddenly I felt the aircraft hit the ground. Nav/Rad. opened the top
hatch and jumped out, I followed a few seconds later and we got about
25 yards away from the aircraft. We sat down and after about half a
minute I saw that both engines were burning at the cylinder heads. I
went back and climbed into the cockpit, switching off all the switches
and looked for the fire extinguisher. I was unable to find it so
gathered handfuls of soil and threw them on to the engines. As most
of the top of the starboard engine cowling had been burnt away, I was
able to put the soil right on the fire in that engine; this seemed
effective and the flames went out. We walked to the nearest road and
were picked up by the ambulance.

On examination of the aircraft later it was discovered that
the engine trouble was caused by both glycol tanks being holed by
debris from the e/a.

CHL Controller.   Fg Off Humphreys.

ARMAMENT REPORT

20 mm. Cannon.   Camera Gun.

Report not available owing   Exposed on second and
to aircraft crashing.   third combats.

J. Singleton, D.F.C. Flt Lt. (Pilot)
....

W.G. Haslam..........Fg Off. (Nav/Rad.).

(Signed) :-   F. BURCHELL   Flt Lt S.I.O.

              for Intelligence Officer
                   25 Squadron.

Map

Annotated by Joe Singleton, with researched positions of '*Three in Thirteen*' engagements.

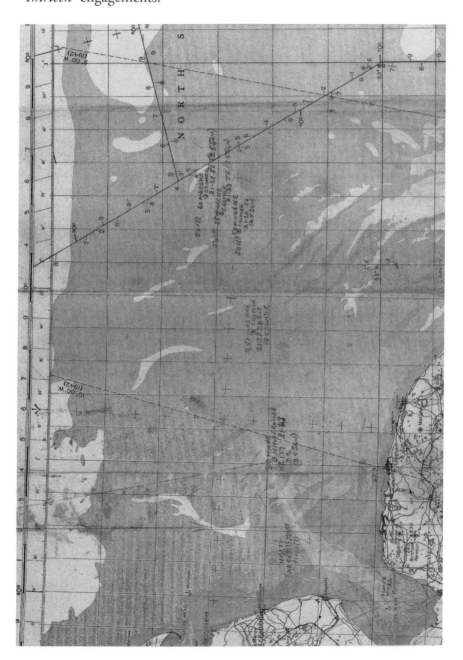

Notes

By Joe Singleton (handwritten and typed) on his recollections of night of 19th March 1944.

Suggested alterations

"Seeing that the engines were burning at the cylinder heads, Singleton returned and switched off petrol & electrical circuits but not being able to locate the fire extinguisher he threw handfuls of soil on to the cylinder heads where burning oil was pouring down the side (the starboard engine cowling had burnt away), this seemed to be effective.

They then walked away from the a/c & came to a road where they were picked up by the station ambulance, taken to sickquarters & treated for slight injuries.

(On examination of the a/c it was apparent that the engine trouble resulted from both glycol tanks being holed by debris from the exploding e/a.)

Next day (20th) A.M. Sir Roderick Hill - C in C Fighter Command flew into Coltishall & discussed and congratulated Singleton & Haslam on the action.

In the late evening of the 20th Stewart-Macpherson, with the B.B.C. outside broadcast team came & interviewed Singleton & Haslam. This was the first time the team had been to a R.A.F. station. The interview was broadcast on the midday (overseas) news the next day (21st)

In mid May the crew were posted to Fighter Command H.Q. prior to taking a N.F. Mosquito to U.S.A. for special duties. Whilst at HQ they managed to borrow a Mosquito from 605 Sqn & shot down a 'Buzz Bomb' over the Channel.

In mid April '44 Singleton was awarded the D.S.O. and Haslam the D.F.C."

"Background notes" - which may be of use.

SINGLETON :-

1. Joined No 25 Sqn Nov '41 until tour expired in June '43   P/o - F/o - Acting F/L - F/L.
'A' Flight. Deputy Flt bdr & Flt bdr
Substantive F/L - May '43.

2. Served at Telecommunications Fighter Unit (DEFFORD) on rest from May 43 to Dec '43.

3. D.F.C. July '43.

'BRAD'
4. From January '42 to Feb 43 my R.O was F/L Bradshaw
H.E. III destroyed in Sept '42 (IN A BEAUFIGHTER) & damaged others during that period.

5. Teamed up with Geoff Harlem in March 43. Shot-down. Ju 88 in Bay of Biscay - day battle - on 13 June 43 (Flying with other R.O" during early '43 also carried out. Ranger & Intruder sorties - mainly trains.

6. In end Dec '43 returned from rest to 'A' Flight - 25 Sqn. Deputy Flt bdr and acting Flt bdr.
Served at Acklington & Coltishall having reteamed with Geoff Harlem.
With my aircraft HK 255 we destroyed :-
   Dornier 217 ── 20 Feb '44
   . Ju 188 ── 14 March '44
   Three Ju 188° ── 19 March 44
(note - this is one more than claimed by Bob Collis on behalf of the aircraft !!)

7. Commanded 25 Sqn April '47 ── Oct '48.
(A.F.C. July '44)   West Malling.

Explanatory Notes for S/L. Guy Woods
(in support of Combat Report for 19 March 44)

Camouflage   Mosquito was, I think, grey all over. I would guess
                            that the German a/c would be green and black.

Armament   Mosquito had 4 - 20 mm. cannon and 6 - 303 m/g'. In
                            the combat report only cannons are mentioned - maybe
                            my m/g' had jammed.

Tracer   Was not used at night. We usually had a mixture of
                            H.E. - A.P. and Incendiary.

Visible Aerials   Probably on E/A.

Control surfaces
mass balances   E/A would have them.

Mosquito Code Letters   "ZK-A".

Mosquito No.   "HK 255"

Weather Conditions   Very black night and not too many stars. There was
                            no moon.

Return Fire   None, all three exploded as per Combat Report. (I am
                            sure none saw us approach.)   The three were
                            Pathfinders carrying marker flares and incendiaries
                            which exploded.

Evasive Action   The Combat Report refers.   The third a/c crew
                            probably saw the explosions, etc. of the first two
                            and so the pilot was corkscrewing violently when we
                            approached.

Reference - manoeuvres - burning - bits falling off - position of combats -
            headings - overtaking - etc.;
                            these are all referred to in my Combat Report. I can
                            only add that it was probably debris from the
                            explosion of the first kill which caused most of the
                            damage to my aircraft.

Fate of Luftwaffe
crews   None would have survived.

Other Information:-

(a)   The target was Hull. The three Pathfinders were spearheading the raid
       and were all sowing DUPEL (Window/Chaff) in large quantities. Geoff
       Haslam did a brilliant job in working through it. With the loss of the
       Pathfinders the raid was a failure as reported by the Yorkshire Evening
       News (I believe on the 20th) that ".....although the size of the raid
       was comparable to those recently attacking London only 75% of the force
       managed to cross the coast....none reached the intended objective and
       only sporadic bombing developed".

(b)   Stuart Macpherson of the B.B.C. came to Coltishall the following
       evening (20th) to interview us. This was broadcast on the midday
       Overseas and National News on the 21st. It was the first time the
       B.B.C. Outside Broadcast team had visited a R.A.F. station.

(c)   The C. in C. Fighter Command, Sir Roderick Hill, flew in to interview
       us on the 20th. This was a very private visit known only to a few on
       the station. Apart from his immediate interest in the combats, he also
       wanted to know how other Nav. Rads. could work through similar window
       conditions, etc.

                                                      J.S.
                                                      20/9/91

Extract

Jack Cheney's diary proof (with annotations by Joe Singleton)
by Alastair Goodrum.

64

3 February.

More lectures and more synthetic training. This is
getting binding and more and more like an O.T.U. and
a lecture on V.D. by the M.O. only helped to add to
that impression.

There was a mild binge this evening and I was able to
win five bob in a beer drinking contest.

4 February.

At long last an opportunity to fly. Joe Singleton took
me up to give me my first taste of the Mosquito and it
was absolutely wizard, nothing to touch it so far. It
is light on the controls, has an excellent stall and
is very good on one engine. Somehow we managed to change
seats while airborne and so at last I took over a
Mosquito. Unfortunately the aircraft went U/S later so
I was unable to go up on my own. Gally went off solo 'm DD 733
in the afternoon and caused quite a stir when he
developed a bad swing on landing which resulted in
a good prang. He wrote off the undercart and damaged
a wingtip, the props and the bomb doors. It would have
been something to smile about except it happened to be
the C.O.'s machine.

In the mess this evening we started up the Uckers board
again and trapped a new sucker in on it.

5 February.

P.T. again, then everyone rushed down to dispersal to see
what cahnce there was of flying. Squadron Leader Carnaby
broke the news that the C.O. had decided that, in view

65

of Gally's fearful efforts we must all have more dual
before being sent off solo. Cries of shame and Gally
is not too popular. I was promised a quick whip around
tomorrow and, as I had already had one trip, I would be
allowed to go off on my own. Bill Mallett and I were
in the Hunt Trainer that same afternoon when the
word went round that Squadron Leader Carnaby and his
Operator, P/O Kemp, had crashed, in Mosquito HJ918 and were both killed.
That was rotten luck, the odd chance in a million and
it had to happen to a really good bloke like Carnaby.

7 February.

Yet more P.T. this morning. Joe Singleton apologised to
me and said he couldn't send me off as the C.O. had put
his foot down very firmly about us having to have more
dual. Bill managed to get in a short trip with Joe but
we are still dogged with unserviceability. Vic flew
down to Wittering presumably to test the Turbinlight
Mosquito.

Mike's commission has come through at last and we were
able to have a few drinks together now that he is with
us in the mess.

2 February.

Bill and I went into Leeds to investigate Squadron Leader
Carnaby's crash. It appears that only two people saw it
and we could track down only one of those. It was in
one sense quite a thrill to go sleuthing around although
our business was pretty grim nevertheless.

Letter

Letter from Chris Goss on Luftwaffe research for night of 19th March 1944.

Mr & Mrs C. H. Goss
37 Trenchard Avenue
West End Road
RUISLIP
Middx HA4 6NP
Tel: (081) 841 3374

20 Feb 94

Dear Joe

My apologies for not writing sooner to thank you for your last letter with its enclosed photocopy and photograph but I have been quite busy and have been away on a course for a week or so.

However, first to the Bay of Biscay. I have written to Heinz Hommel saying that you would like to meet him but as yet, I have heard nothing. I have also had a lot more luck contacting a few more Mossie crews who got German ac in 1943—one chap was quite amazed to be told he had shot one down having only claimed a damaged! I am waiting for photos from the widow of the German pilot (he survived but died in 1984) which will interest the RAF pilot alot!

Now to your kills on 19-20 Mar 44. I have ascertained that the attack was against Hull and that the German units involved were KG 2, KG 30, KG 54, KG 100 with the pathfinder unit being KG 66. Ju 88/188/He 177 losses I have managed to work out so far are:

KG 66: Lost the pathfinder leader which crashed off the Humber Estuary. I am being sent a photocopy of the original loss report which I will send to you as this is one of the ac you must have got.

KG 30: II/KG 30 lost 4 ac but I need to investigate this further.

KG 54: Lost Ju 88 A-4, serial 142293 coded B3+CH of 1/KG 54. Lt Ferdinand Stadtmueller, Unteroffiziers (Uffz) Willi Boderke, Rudolf Haman and Walter Plate missing.

KG 100: 2/KG 100 lost He 177 A-3, serial 2375 coded 6N+OK. Oblt Heinrich Mueller, Ogefr Fritz Kuechler, Uffz Ernst Guendner, Uffz Eberhard Hockauff, Uffz Heinrich Rodenstein and Ogefr Werner Utikal all missing.

For interest, KG 2 (who operated Ju 188s and Do 217s) lost a Do 217 to Flt Lt Greaves of 25 Sqn—one Ju 188 was damaged by fighters.

So, without looking up who else shot down ac that night, this might give you an idea of who you might have got!

Hoping that this is of interest

Kindest wishes to you and the family

Notes

Prologue

1 Winston Churchill, *The Second World War: Volume V – Closing The Ring*, London 1948 – referring to the Battle of the Atlantic.
2 Two aircraft in echelon either side of the leader and sub-leader.
3 Firing about 70 degrees inside the direct line of sight.
4 Chris Goss, *Bloody Biscay*, Crecy Publishing, Manchester, 1997.

Chapter 1. From Paints to Pay Parades

1 *London Gazette* citation: 'In May, 1941, during the enemy advance in Libya, this officer performed splendid work in conveying vital information to the various commanders. During the action he landed beside a battery of artillery which, by his timely warning, was able to move to a better position. Flight Lieutenant McFall displayed outstanding gallantry and devotion to duty throughout a difficult period.'
2 Joe frequently states in his correspondence that he volunteered for the RAF on the Wednesday following outbreak of war. Since he arrived at Padgate on the Thursday, it is unclear whether he undertook his selection procedure on 6th September at some location other than Padgate, or on Day 1 of Reception.
3 M. Bailey, *Evolution of Aptitude Testing*, Cranwell, 1999.
4 Air Historical Branch Narrative – Pre-War Expansion – Training.
5 AHB Narrative.
6 Denoting trainee aircrew.
7 Terence Kelly, *Nine Lives of a Fighter Pilot*, Crowood Press, 2005.
8 Kelly, *Nine Lives of a Fighter Pilot*.
9 Winston Churchill, *The Second World War: Volume II – Their Finest Hour*, London, 1948.

Chapter 2. Out of the Nest, into the Night

1   A one-piece, padded flying suit, named after Sidney Cotton, WWI RNAS pilot who developed it.
2   Geoffrey Wellum, *First Light, New York*, Viking Books, 2002; London, Penguin Books 2003.
3   'The Few', House of Commons, 20 August 1940. *Winston Churchill's Speeches – Never Give In!* Pimlico 2007.
4   'QFI' is awarded on graduation from the Central Flying School (CFS). The demand for instructors became so great during WWII that the requirement to attend CFS to become an instructor was waived; it was reinstated in 1945.
5   Wellum, *First Light, New York*.
6   Chuchill, 'The Few', *Winston Churchill's Speeches – Never Give In!*
7   Churchill, *The Second World War: Volume II – Their Finest Hour.*

Chapter 3. Creamed Off

1   Bill Gunston, *Night Fighter – A Development and Combat History*, The History Press, 2004.
2   *Ibid.*
3   Lewis Brandon, *Night Flyer*, Goodall Publications, 1999.
4   Twin-engined RAF heavy bomber, unsuccessful precursor to the Lancaster.
5   Hitler's Operation *Barbarossa* to invade Russia began on 22 June 1941.

Chapter 4. Front Line at Last – Where's the Action?

1   William James (Marmaduke) Alington 'Marmie'. Son of Lieutenant Colonel Arthur Cyril Marmaduke Alington (1872–1930), and Gladys Evelyn Hamilton (1883–1971), of Binbrook, Lincolnshire. Later AFC DFC and bar.
2   Lord Rothmere, proprietor of the *Daily Mail*, expressed an interest for a private business aircraft and provided funding, totalling £18,500 for its development. He later gifted it to the RAF for further development.
3   Using on-board radio direction-finding equipment to home to the overhead of an airfield and fly an outbound/inbound descending pattern, to end up lined up with the runway at a few hundred feet. Determining the precise overhead was difficult as the radio beacon only transmitted horizontally – the ATC controller would go outside, listen for the aircraft noise and fire a rocket when he judged the aircraft to be overhead... Later evolved into a 'QGH' approach.
4   Harold Chalton Bradshaw (15th February 1893–15th October 1943) was a Liverpool-born architect. His design work included the British School at Rome's Common Room (1924, as projected by Edwin Lutyens) and several Commonwealth War Graves Commission First World War cemeteries and

memorials, including the Cambrai Memorial in France and the Ploegsteert Memorial to the Missing and its surrounding cemetery. He also designed the Guards' Division Memorial in St. James's Park in London, the left-hand sculpted figure of which, coincidentally, bears the name Sgt R Bradshaw MM – any connection is unknown.

5   British scientists invented the cavity magnetron early in 1940. This was a small device that generated microwave frequencies more efficiently than previous devices, allowing the development of practical (small, light) centimetric (wavelength under one metre) radar. This allowed for the detection of much smaller objects and the use of much smaller antennas than the earlier lower frequency sets. The cavity magnetron was perhaps the single most important invention in the history of radar and played a major part in the Allies' victory. In September 1940, the invention was given free to the U.S., who went on to develop the Mk X AI radar from it – (see Chap 9).

6   Located at RAF Ford W Sussex, now the open prison. Joe was to get to know the FIU well later in the war.

7   Brandon, *Night Flyer.*

Chapter 5. Finally into the Fight

1   Usually a light aircraft used for non-operational transport/communications purposes.

2   Similar to Joe's Mk I, but with greater armament capacity.

3   Covering north-west England, parent organisation for 255 Squadron.

4   On the Yorkshire coast near Spurn Head. Probably a mobile radar with Trollope sitting in a caravan equipped with radar screen and radio. The radar was effective down to no less than 500ft and would form part of the Ground Controlled Interception (CGI) system which was 25 Squadron's more usual modus operandi.

5   Awarded MC and OBE, was the first OC of the School of Fighter Control (52–54). Retired as Group Captain 1966.

6   Near Skegness, Lincolnshire.

Chapter 6. Enter the Mossie

1   Widely quoted, but of unconfirmed provenance.

2   The first prototypes were built in a barn at Salisbury Hall, Colney, where the de Havilland designers were secretly ensconced. Salisbury Hall – built in the 1600s and famed for being the location of liaisons between Charles II and Nell Gwynne – is a couple of miles from what is now South Mimms Service Station and currently houses the de Havilland Heritage Aircraft Centre, including the Mosquito Museum. The prototype parts were then transported a few miles up the

A1 to RAF Hatfield for assembly and first flight, by Sir Geoffrey de Havilland himself.

3   Brandon, *Night Flyer.*

4   25 Squadron's aircraft, for some time to come were fitted with the Mk IV or Mk V AI, with aerials scattered around the wings and fuselage, allowing retention of the four Brownings. Later, when the AI Mk VIII arrived, fitted into a thimble radome in the nose, the Browning were removed and the only armament were the Hispanos.

5   Henry Erskine Bodien was to become another Mosquito Ace with five kills on 151 Squadron being awarded DSO and DFC.

Chapter 7. From Defence to Attack

1   Luftwaffe fighter base in Eastern occupied Netherlands, near border with Germany.

2   Common deception technique used by Luftwaffe, usually known to British Intelligence and briefed to crews.

3   Just over the border into Germany, Rheine was another Luftwaffe fighter base. Joe has penetrated Germany!

4   Approach aid using Morse code indicating an aircraft's position relative to the runway centre-line. Later in the form of radio signals audible in the cockpit, early 'Visual' Lorenz worked on the same principle using lights.

5   At the end of its landing run, two thirds of the way down the runway.

6   Syke, Heiligenrode and Bassum are small towns to the south of Bremen, north Germany.

7   Royal Canadian Air Force, though crews would be drawn from countries other than Canada.

8   Nightfighter Navigator E. G. White OBE.

9   Flown by Joe and Geoff H 10th and 11th March 1943 for A-A and A-S firing practice.

10 With strengthened wings to carry two 500lb bombs on pylons.

Chapter 8. A Cornish Interlude

1   Extract from RAF Museum timeline document for 1943.

2   So named because the President of Madras personally financed equipping Squadron with Defiants in 1938.

3   Disguises an intense high-level struggle between Bomber Harris and John Slessor (Commander-in-Chief Coastal Command) for priority in the use of Mosquitos for support. Churchill, rather belatedly seeing the anti-U-boat Campaign at tipping point, finally over-rules Harris and lets Slessor have some Mosquitos – but only temporarily.

4   Especially the large FW 200 Condor – a four-engined bomber/recce aircraft converted from an airliner.

5   Brandon, *Night Flyer,* p 112 et seq.

6   2 and 3 in echelon either side of the leader.

7   Two pilots from 13/KG 40 reported combats with Mossies on 11th June 1943. Uffz Heinz Hommel took off from Lorient at 1629 hrs and landed 2209 hrs whilst Lieutenant Knud Gmelin took off at 1331 hrs and landed 1740 hrs. Joe's claim was 1620 hrs, Wootton of 25 Squadron claimed a damaged at 1615 hrs whilst Newell of 456 Squadron damaged another two at 1617 hrs. My guess is that Hommel's section was taking over from Gmelin's when they encountered the Mosquitos (Chris Goss, in correspondence).

8   Firing about 70 degrees inside the direct line of sight.

9   Goss, *Bloody Biscay.*

Chapter 9. An Exhausting Rest

1   Then a commodore and Chief of Combined Operations.

2   Showers of metallised paper strips dropped from aircraft to cause multiple radar returns, masking a target within it –a technology effectively used for many decades afterwards. Called 'chaff' by the US at the time, the UK would follow that terminology after the war.

3   Joe carries out several tests on 'squint' – a signal strength problem producing a false indication of position.

4   Probably known by the ground operators as 'Beam' because they were sending out a beam for aircrew to follow, and by aircrew as 'Blind' because it enabled them to make a blind (i.e. on instruments alone) approach.

5   BABS equipment clearly had reliability issues. On 22nd July, Joe records: 'BABS – Beacon working!'

6   Most likely Signals Intelligence Unit.

7   RAF standard practice was for the ground crew to assist passengers to strap in. RN ground crew probably saw them off and their procedures were perhaps different – Joe did not check.

Chapter 10. Three in Thirteen

1   High-altitude (pressurised) variant with bigger wings, more powerful (RR Merlin 76) engines and an electronic counter-measures suite – final version of Mosquito, prior to the end of the war. Note change from Roman to Arabic numerals, which was occurring with all RAF aircraft to bring them in line with US terminology.

2   The squadron that wrote off one of 25's dual-control Mosquitos at Coleby Grange in June 1943.

3   Almost all traces of the airfield are now gone. The runways have been dug up for open-cast coal mining and the hangars are now part of an open prison.

4   Pronounced '*haze bruh*' – on the north Norfolk coast near Cromer.

5   Although in use with night fighter squadrons for some months, this was the first occasion Joe had benefitted from them. Geoff had probably been using them for some time. Developed originally at Stanford University, Ca USA it was the forerunner of Night Vision Goggles (NVG).

6   Exercises designed to simulate as closely as possible real operational scenarios. Most likely, on this occasion practice intercepts, perhaps on bombers on training sorties. Bomber, fighter and controller would all benefit.

7   Retired as Squadron Leader with nine kills, DFC and Bar. Ran family printing business in Scarborough after the war. Died 2006, aged 89.

8   At RAF Watnall north-west of Nottingham, which covered central and northern England.

9   The positions of all three engagements are reported differently in different reports. The best information, using Luftwaffe as well as RAF data, is plotted on map at Appendix.

10 Upwards facing lights on the ground to 'funnel' pilots on to the runway centre-line.

11 It was normal practice in war to land without lights – lesson from Intruder Operations. Here he is no longer concerned he may be seen by a German, more that he would like to see the ground and cushion the landing … but as it relied on aircraft power he no longer had, it was very slow in deploying.

12 Coolant. Joe retrieved and for many years kept a lump of Bakelite-type material from the 188 embedded in his aircraft.

13 The Luftwaffe's only attempt to produce a long-range bomber, which proved to be something of a disaster.

14 The pathfinders, who would have been the most skilled crews with the best navigational equipment available, flew at the front of the bomber stream. Their job was to find the target and mark it with flares and/or incendiaries so the less capable bombers behind would have the best possible chance of hitting the target.

15 In Imperial War Museum archives.

16 Ron Mackay and Simon W. Parry, *'The Last Blitz' Operation Steinbock*, Red Kite 2011.

Chapter 11. Aftermath

1   An outlier of the Bentley Priory HQ.

Bibliography

Air Historical Branch Narrative.

Bailey, M., *Evolution of Aptitude Testing*, Cranwell, 1999.

Brandon, Lewis, *Night Flyer*, Goodall Publications, 1999.

Churchill, Winston, *The Second World War Vols 1–6*, London, 1948.

Goss, Chris, *Bloody Biscay*, Crecy Publishing, Manchester, 1997.

Goodrum, Alastair, *Jack Cheney's Diary*, Flypast Magazine, 1988.

Gunston, Bill, *Night Fighter – A Development and Combat History*, The History Press, 2004.

Kelly, Terence, *Nine Lives of a Fighter Pilot*, Crowood Press, 2005.

Mackay, Ron and Parry, Simon W., *'The Last Blitz' Operation Steinbock*, Red Kite 2011.

Wellum, Geoffrey, *First Light, New York*, Viking Books, 2002; London, Penguin Books 2003.

White, E. G., *Nightfighter Navigator*, Thurlestone, Devon, 1994.